Success with Chinese
A Communicative Approach for Beginners

READING & WRITING

De-an Wu Swihart

CHENG & TSUI COMPANY
Boston

10 09 08 07 06 05   8 7 6 5 4 3 2 1

Published by
Cheng & Tsui Company, Inc.
25 West Street
Boston, MA 02111-1213 USA
Fax (617) 426-3669
www.cheng-tsui.com
"Bringing Asia to the World"™

ISBN 0-88727-475-7

Library of Congress Cataloging-in-Publication Data
Swihart, De-an Wu
Success with Chinese : a communicative approach for beginners / by De-an Wu Swihart.
        p.   cm.
Includes index.
ISBN 0-88727-425-0 (pbk.)
  2. Chinese language—Textbooks for foreign speakers—English. I. Title.
PL1129.E5S95 2004
495.1'82421—dc22

                                        2004063502

Printed in the U.S.A.

Publisher's Note

The Cheng & Tsui Asian Language Series is designed to publish and widely distribute quality language learning materials created by leading instructors from around the world. We welcome readers' comments and suggestions concerning the publications in this series. Please send feedback to our Editorial Department (e-mail: editor@cheng-tsui.com), or contact the following members of our Editorial Board.

Professor Shou-hsin Teng, *Chief Editor*
3 Coach Lane, Amherst, MA 01002

Professor Dana Scott Bourgerie
Asian and Near Eastern Languages, Brigham Young University, Provo, UT 84602

Professor Samuel Cheung
Dept. of Chinese, Chinese University of Hong Kong, Shatin, Hong Kong

Professor Ying-che Li
Dept. of East Asian Languages, University of Hawaii, Honolulu, HI 96822

Professor Timothy Light
Dept. of Comparative Religion, Western Michigan University, Kalamazoo, MI 49008

Abbreviations

Abbreviation	English	Pinyin	Chinese
Adj	Adjective	xíngróngcí	形容词
Adv	Adverb	fùcí	副词
Aux	Auxiliary	zhùdòngcí	助动词
Conj	Conjunction	liáncí	连词
Exp	Expression	xíguàn yòngyǔ	习惯用语
Int	Interrogative	yíwèncí	疑问词
Intj	Interjection	tàncí	叹词
Meas	Measure Word	liàngcí	量词
N	Noun	míngcí	名词
Num	Numeral	shùcí	数词
Part	Particle	zhùcí	助词
Prep	Proposition	jiècí	介词
Pron	Pronoun	dàimíngcí	代词
PropN	Proper Noun	zhuānyǒu míngcí	专有名词
V	Verb	dòngcí	动词
VO	Verb-object	dòngbīn jiégòu	动宾结构

Contents

Introduction vii

READING & WRITING

1   Chinese Characters 3

2   Numbers 13

3   Money (1) 21

4   Money (2) 29

5   Foods 37

6   Tastes & Cooking Methods 45

7   Cutting Methods & Kinds of Food 53

8   Drinks 63

9   Reading Menus 71

10 Telephone 81

11 Hotels 91

12 Signs & Directions (1) 99

13 Signs & Directions (2) 107

14 Signs & Directions (3) 117

15 Time (1) 127

16 Time (2) 137

17 Calendars 147

18 Filling in Forms 157

Appendix I: Radical List by Lesson 167

Appendix II: List of Radicals 173

Appendix III: Vocabulary List 177

Introduction

The Proficiency Guidelines developed by the American Council for the Teaching of Foreign Languages (ACTFL) in 1986 provide global measurement of integrated performance in speaking, listening, reading, and writing a foreign language. The establishment of those Proficiency Guidelines reflects a significant change in the contemporary direction of foreign language teaching, with less emphasis on single methodologies, and an increased focus on the end results of language learning. In this way, a variety of methods, approaches, materials and curricula are oriented toward one goal—proficiency. The advantages of such an approach have been particularly evident to me in ten years of taking students to Beijing for summer study and in seven years of preparing English speakers to live in China. Whenever learners can apply their classroom knowledge to a real-life conversation, their learning is powerfully reinforced and their motivation is strengthened. All learners of Chinese language profit from instructional methods that are context-based and culture-centered, with an ultimate emphasis beyond the classroom, on day-to-day natural language usage. There is a need for Chinese language textbooks that can bridge the gap between what is taught in the classroom and what is spoken by native speakers every day.

Five years ago, in response to the lack of materials for teaching practical Chinese language for everyday communication, I began writing context-based, proficiency-oriented teaching materials to train beginning students from the ACTFL OPI (Oral Proficiency Interview) novice level (students can produce mainly isolated words and phrases) to the intermediate level (students can function in sentence-length discourse, using appropriate connector and transitional phrases). *Success with Chinese* takes a unique proficiency-based approach and has been field tested in both China and the United States.

With its up-to-date, real-life situations based in China, this book fills a clear need for context-based learning. Its wide use of authentic daily language contexts helps students make rapid progress in speaking, listening, reading, and writing in Chinese for preparation to live, study, work, or travel in China.

How This Book's Design Leads to Success with Chinese

This book was written for people who plan to live or work in China—students, English teachers, and others. It can also be used as a textbook in regular college courses, in immersion programs, in intensive summer programs, and in language training schools.

Success with Chinese is structured in two separate but coordinated parts: Listening & Speaking and Reading & Writing. This is because the phonetic language background of English speakers leads them to expect to be able to look at an unfamiliar word and determine its pronunciation from its spelling. But Chinese, as a character-based, non-phonetic language, does not allow that, except through Pinyin, the Chinese system for phonetically transliterating Chinese characters into the Latin alphabet. Thus the task of learning a Chinese character entails learning the graphic character, its meaning, and its Pinyin pronunciation, both spelling and tone. Very often, English speakers learn to speak and understand Chinese faster than they learn to read and write it. Most students need time to learn to connect the pronunciation of Chinese characters with their shapes, and only then can they read.

This use of a coordinated two-part structure allows teachers, as well as individual learners, considerable flexibility in designing the instruction and learning process.

- Students can learn Chinese by studying the two parts concurrently, but without having to use the same pace for Listening & Speaking as for Reading & Writing. It is recommended to have students concentrate primarily on speaking and listening at first, while learning reading and writing at a slower pace. This allows students, especially native speakers of English, to have more confidence about learning Chinese, because they will already have learned to say many of the words by the time they are asked to learn the Chinese characters.

- For students who wish to learn only spoken Chinese, Listening & Speaking may be studied independently of Reading & Writing. For students who are learning or who have already learned some spoken Chinese, Reading & Writing can be used as an independent course.

- In the Chinese dialogues and short passages in this book, Pinyin transliterations are printed directly below each Chinese character, rather than in a separate section away from the characters, as is commonly done in many Chinese textbooks. This design helps English speakers associate the Chinese characters with their sounds. I believe that in this way, an English-speaking student of Chinese will make the connection between characters and sounds more quickly and will later learn to read characters without the help of Pinyin.

The lessons in Listening & Speaking are thematically coordinated with the lessons in Reading & Writing. The former opens with an introduction to Pinyin and pronunciation; the latter opens with an introduction to Chinese characters. Thereafter, the coordination between the two parts is according to the context-based modules, as follows:

Listening & Speaking		*Reading & Writing*
Lesson(s)	Topic of Module	Lesson(s)
2	Numbers	2
3	Money	3–4
4–5	Food	5–9
6	Telephone	10
7	Hotels	11
8	Directions	12–14
9–10	Time, Schedules, & Forms	15–18

The characters selected for inclusion in Reading & Writing do not simply mirror the vocabulary lists in Listening & Speaking. Instead, they are the characters that are most relevant to daily life in China and are commonly seen on signs, menus, schedules, etc. In teaching large numbers of Americans who are spending a year in China while learning Chinese, I have found that this approach is especially useful to those people who want to quickly learn how to find their way around China. To them, learning Chinese characters is a matter of survival. At the same time, the book meets the needs of all students, and the selected characters are also the foundation for a program in academic reading, as I will explain later.

How the Lessons Are Organized

The Listening & Speaking Component

Training students to speak well and to understand what native speakers say is the most important task of a foreign language teacher. The Listening & Speaking portion of *Success with Chinese* employs a variety of teaching methods to help students achieve oral proficiency.

Lesson One introduces the Pinyin system and the pronunciation of standard Chinese. Each of the other nine lessons is a module focused on a daily life situation such as counting numbers, exchanging money, eating at a restaurant, making a telephone call, and asking directions—practical topics that are directly relevant to daily life and that can therefore motivate the student to learn. The first module is the immediately useful skill of counting numbers. Greetings, with which most Chinese textbooks begin, can wait until Lesson Three. The arrangement of vocabulary and grammar topics is from simple to complex, although occasionally a departure is needed to familiarize students with a situation that will be immediately useful to them.

This book starts with *shǔ shù* (counting numbers), rather than with teaching the greeting *nǐ hǎo* (hello), as do most Chinese textbooks. During three years of using the topics and vocabulary in this book with beginning students both in China and in the United States, we have found that because of the obvious usefulness of the topics, students are particularly interested in them, and with that motivation they are willing to work harder and can learn faster and more effectively.

Starting with Lesson Two, each lesson opens with a list of **Key Expressions** that introduces important words and phrases from that lesson's dialogues. The two **Dialogues** in each lesson were created based on research into the frequency of usage for the specific situation in daily life. While the language found in the dialogues is used in daily life in China, it is appropriately simple for beginners. Each dialogue has accompanying notes, a vocabulary list, and an English translation. The dialogues, which reflect a variety of specific daily situations, allow learners to communicate with native Chinese speakers in a realistic environment. Students should master the dialogues and try to create their own dialogues based on the situations.

The **Grammar Notes** are linked to the dialogues. The explanations are written from the angle of how English speakers see Chinese grammar, and comparisons with English are used extensively. For example, a grammar note in Lesson Nine points out that the word order of 以前 yǐqián (before) or 以后 yǐhòu (after) in a Chinese sentence is the reverse of that in English, where "before" or "after" precedes a time or event. In Chinese they follow a time or event word, so that the English "before 11:00" and "after class" become, respectively, "11:00 以前 yǐqián" (literally, 11:00 before) and "下课以后 xiàkè yǐhòu" (literally, class after).

The dialogues include sentence patterns that have been selected because they are commonly used in daily life in China and illustrate the grammar points of that lesson. The sentence patterns are of central importance in helping students learn conversational Chinese. The **Grammar Practice & Sentence Patterns** section of each lesson provides a diagram of each sentence pattern, with the sentence elements in separate blocks. Remembering the correct position of each block in a sentence pattern will help students make new sentences with that pattern. Drills using the sentence patterns foster students' ability to make their own sentences, so they can begin to engage in conversations with others.

Like the Grammar Notes, the **Pronunciation Notes** and the **Pronunciation Exercises** are chosen and designed specifically for English speakers, emphasizing pronunciation of the sounds that are new to them. Each lesson has **Listening Comprehension Exercises**, which train students to understand native speakers, **Communication Activities**, which train students to make sentences in Chinese and foster their ability to understand and respond to what is being said in daily conversations, and ***Review Exercises***. At the end of each lesson are notes on ***Understanding Chinese Culture*** relevant to the content of the lesson. These notes provide cultural and practical information about China that is interesting to students and that can help them understand and use the language.

The Reading & Writing Component

The Reading & Writing portion of *Success with Chinese* opens with an "Introduction to Chinese Characters," which explains the general rules of character writing, beginning with the types of strokes and emphasizing the importance of the order of strokes. Students are also introduced to the structure of a character. The subsequent seventeen lessons each introduce twelve to eighteen characters. The characters are listed at the beginning of each lesson in a table that shows each character with its Pinyin pronunciation and its meaning(s). This format emphasizes that each Chinese character can be an independent unit.

Each lesson includes a ***Learning Radicals*** section, which is an important element in the design of this textbook. Learning radicals is a very powerful aid to students learning Chinese characters. Each lesson teaches four radicals. A standard list of 227 radicals from the *Modern Chinese Dictionary* (*Xiàndài Hànyǔ Cídiǎn* 现代汉语词典) is provided in an appendix. Students should practice and memorize the radicals so that they are able to recognize them when they see a new Chinese character.

Then comes an analysis of the ***Structure*** of each character, showing its components and radicals, which are its building blocks. Students are expected to remember each character and to be able to pronounce it, write it, and know its meaning as a single character, as well as being alert to the changes of its meaning when it is in a compound with other characters.

Next, there are from three to five ***Reading Practice*** exercises that use repetition and character compound analysis to build students' ability to recognize new words that combine characters they have already learned. The last section of each lesson is ***Writing Practice,*** which provides illustrations of the stroke order for each new character. Students must practice writing Chinese characters in order to remember them. I suggest that students be tested on five Chinese characters in every class meeting.

The Effectiveness of a Proficiency-Based Approach to Reading

Training students to read Chinese is an important stepping stone for them in learning to write Chinese. *Success with Chinese* places heavy emphasis on reading and uses a variety of practices to teach reading.

Students Learn through Repetition

Because Western education usually places more emphasis on analysis than on memorization, English speakers often are not well practiced in mechanical memorization. The reading exercises in Reading & Writing are designed to help students learn Chinese characters through repetition. Each new character is listed with examples of its use in several compound words. This shows students how learning one character will help them learn many new words that use the character in compounds. The students also see that a character can have various meanings when it is in a compound. The character is then repeated elsewhere in the lesson and is further reinforced by repetition in later lessons. Just as seeing a picture over and over makes it become familiar, repetition of a character will lead students to recognize and remember it.

Students Learn through Character Analysis

In *Success with Chinese,* there are reading exercises that ask students to analyze the meaning of compounds and short phrases, as for example when reading the names of dishes on a Chinese menu. For instance, in Reading & Writing Lessons Five through Nine, students learn how to analyze the names of many dishes on a Chinese menu after learning only sixty-two characters carefully selected from five basic groups:

a. Food categories (rice, noodles, fried bread, steamed bread, soup, etc.)

b. Ingredients (chicken, pork, beef, fish, shrimp, vegetable, eggs, etc.)

c. Tastes (sweet, sour, spicy, etc.)

d. Cooking methods (stir-fry, stew, boil, steam, cold mix, etc.)

e. Shapes (strips, chunks, diced cubes, slices, threadlike pieces, etc.).

The names of Chinese dishes on a menu usually combine elements from these five groups. For example, "chǎo làzi jī dīng 炒辣子鸡丁" is stir-fried spicy diced chicken, and "suān là tāng 酸辣汤" is a hot-and-sour soup. When students master these sixty-two characters and learn how to analyze character combinations, they can confidently use a Chinese restaurant menu, even though they will not understand the names of the dishes. This same approach is used in exercises that teach the reading of signs, street names, schedules, and many other documents that students will encounter. The practical use of Chinese characters will reinforce students' memory of them.

Students Understand Chinese Sentence Structure

Reading words and phrases on menus and signs is the first step in learning to read Chinese, and it is relatively easy for English speakers. But Chinese sentences and paragraphs can be difficult because there are no spaces between the words in a sentence in Chinese publications. Since a word can range in length from a single character to as many as four characters, it takes practice for non-native speakers to determine the word divisions. For example, when I took students out in Beijing to let them try to read signs, one sign they saw read, "dàxuéshēng huódòng zhōngxīn 大学生 活动中心" (College Students' Activity Center). One student incorrectly separated "College" (大学 dàxué) from "College Students" (大学生 dàxuéshēng) and thus wrongly guessed, "It's the name of a college."

To help students develop reading skills, Reading & Writing begins with exercises in reading short units and then moves to increasingly longer units. Students start by reading characters, then progress to words, then phrases, then sentences in Lesson Eight, and finally short paragraphs in Lessons Fourteen through Eighteen. Each lesson has a section that asks students to find the characters they recognize in a short essay. It is like a "Where's Waldo" game, and it helps students review the characters they have already learned, while becoming familiar with how words are divided in printed Chinese. By doing these exercises, students will gradually attain an academic classroom reading level, and they will also have gained considerable confidence and motivation because they first learned to read signs, menus, and schedules in daily life.

About the Author

De-an Wu Swihart wrote and designed all of Book 2: Reading & Writing. She is a graduate of the Chinese Department of Beijing University and received a Ph.D. from Princeton University. She has published three books. She has been teaching Chinese language and literature in the United States and Canada since 1990, and is currently Co-Director of the Center for Teaching & Learning in China LLC, Memphis, Tennessee.

Success with Chinese

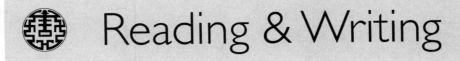

Reading & Writing

Chinese Characters

第 一 课　汉 字

Dì yī kè　　　　*Hànzì*

This lesson introduces you to Chinese characters.

The evolution of Chinese characters
Simplified and complex forms of Chinese characters
Strokes of Chinese characters
Stroke order
The structure of Chinese characters
Radicals
Practice identifying the strokes, stroke order, and character structure
Practice writing the strokes

English writing is phonetic, but the Chinese writing system is non-phonetic and uses ideograph symbols called "Hànzì" (汉字 Chinese characters). Because the shape of a Chinese character does not represent its sound, learners with a phonetic language background initially find Chinese more difficult to learn because they cannot sound out Chinese characters. Some characters do have a component that suggests the pronunciation, but those sound components have never been systematically developed. The first officially accepted Chinese phonetic system for the standard pronunciation of Chinese characters was called the National Phonetic Alphabet (zhùyīn zìmǔ), which was developed during the "Phonetic Alphabet Movement" (Qièyīnzì yùndòng) that took place from 1892 to 1919. Since that time there have been more than twenty Chinese phonetic alphabets created. Pinyin is the latest standard phonetic system for Mandarin pronunciation of Chinese characters. Phonetic language background students have to learn the pronunciation of characters through Pinyin, as well as learn the shape of the characters and their meanings. Therefore students need extra time to learn to connect the pronunciation of Chinese characters with their graphic shapes. Pinyin is a useful tool to help learn Chinese characters, but it is only a tool for learning to read Chinese characters more rapidly. Students need to gradually learn to read Chinese characters directly, without the help of the Pinyin phonetic versions of the characters. Notice also that many Chinese words that have different characters are homophones, that is, they are identical in sound. Thus they are identical in Pinyin, even though the difference is clear in the characters themselves. For example, "yī" can mean "one" (一) or "clothes" (衣) or "doctor" (医).

THE EVOLUTION OF CHINESE CHARACTERS

Chinese characters have gradually developed from their beginnings as pictorial symbols into straight-line, square-shaped forms. The long history of the evolution of Chinese characters can be roughly divided into three stages. The first stage was from oracle bone inscriptions to "small seal" script (fourteenth century BC–207 BC). The oracle bone inscriptions (jiǎgǔwén 甲骨文), which are the earliest surviving Chinese characters, were found on tortoise shells and animal bones from the fourteenth century BC, and on some pottery found two centuries earlier. These archaic characters were pictorial symbols, and because they were written on animal bones, shells, and bamboo, their forms were rough.

The second step was from "small seal" script to "official script." During the Qin dynasty (211–207 BC) a more artistic script was created called "xiǎozhuàn" (小篆 small seal script), which was used as a standard script. Later a simplified version called "lìshū" (隶书) became the official script in the Han dynasty (206 BC–220 AD).

The third stage was "regular script" called "Kǎishū" (楷书), which was created during the Wei and Jin dynasties (220–420 AD). Kǎishū became a standard in printing and continues to be used today. The following chart shows the development of the characters:

Archaic form	Modern form	Meaning
亻	人	man, person
⩎	山	mountain
⊙	日	sun
⊃	月	moon

Simplified and Complex Forms of Chinese Characters

Another aspect in the development of Chinese characters is the introduction of simplified forms. From ancient times, there were two co-existing forms of character writing: the traditional or "official" form (zhèngtǐzì 正体字) that used complex forms of characters, and the "unofficial" form (sútǐzì 俗体字) that used simplified forms of characters. The traditional official forms of Chinese characters, which can have as many as thirty-three separate strokes, were overly complex both for writers and learners. In 1956, a Character Reform Committee was formed to systematically simplify Chinese characters. This committee, made up of Chinese linguists, collected and collated the simplified, unofficial forms of characters used by people in daily life. The reformers then further simplified the most frequently used characters, reducing the number of strokes by an average of one half. Lists of simplified Chinese characters were introduced, leading to the publication in 1964 of *A Conversion Table of Simplified Chinese Characters*, later revised in 1986. It contains 2,235 simplified Chinese characters that now are the official form. Here are some examples:

Pinyin	Complex form	Simplified form
mā	媽	妈
yuán	圓	圆
hàn	漢	汉

Simplified characters are used in all books, newspapers, and magazines in China. However, Taiwan still uses the complex characters. This textbook uses simplified characters because it is designed for learners living in China.

STROKES OF CHINESE CHARACTERS

Strokes are the basic components of Chinese characters. Eight basic stroke types are used in writing Chinese characters:

Stroke name		Stroke Direction	Example
1. Horizontal stroke (橫 héng)	一	From left to right	二
2. Vertical stroke (竖 shù)	丨	From top to bottom	中
3. Left downward stroke (撇 piě)	丿	From top-right to bottom-left	人
4. Right downward stroke (捺 nà)	㇏	From top-left to bottom-right	八
5. Dot (diǎn 点)	丶	left dot, right dot	小
	灬	bottom dot	点
6. Strokes with a hook (钩 gōu): Gōu is not an independent stroke; it is formed with other strokes.		Form the hook at the end of the stroke by quickly making a turn and then lifting the brush.	
Left vertical hook	亅		丁
Right vertical hook	乚		也
Horizontal hook	乛		买
Arm-hook	勹		勺
Right downward bending hook	乙		戈
Dragon-tail hook	弋		九
7. Turning stroke (折 zhé)	フ	Horizontal line first, then turn	又
	ㄥ	Vertical line first, then turn	区
	㇄		山
	く	Left-downward first then right-downward	女
8. Rising stroke (提 tí)	╱	From bottom-left rising up	冲

Stroke Order

The following rules for the order of strokes should be followed carefully when writing Chinese characters. They make writing faster and easier, and also help in learning the characters.

1. From top to bottom

If a character contains two or more stokes, complete the top one first and then the bottom. If a character contains two or more parts, complete the top part first (the top stroke still goes first), then the middle, and then the bottom parts.

毛　ノ → 三 → 毛

分　ノ → 八 → 分

上　丨 → 卜 → 上

2. From left to right

If a character contains two or more strokes, complete the left stroke first, then the middle, and then the right. If a character contains two or three parts, complete the left part first (the stroke order is still from top to bottom and left to right in each part), then the middle, and then the right.

人　ノ → 人

什　亻 → 仁 → 什

谁　讠 → 讠 → 谁

3. Horizontal strokes first, then vertical strokes

干　一 → 二 → 干

万　一 → 丁 → 万

曼　日 → 𣊫 → 曼

4. Center stroke first, then left and right strokes

小　亅 → 刂 → 小

子　𠃌 → 了 → 子

水　亅 → 刁 → 水

5. Outside first, then inside

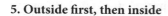

月　　丿 → 刀 → 月

问　　丶 → 门 → 问

风　　丿 → 几 → 风

6. Fill up before closing

回　　冂 → 冋 → 回

国　　冂 → 国 → 国

园　　冂 → 园 → 园

THE STRUCTURE OF CHINESE CHARACTERS

Some Chinese characters are single-structured, but most of the characters are composed of two or more components. The following are the four basic structures of Chinese characters.

1. *Single structure*

毛

máo (¥0.10)

2. a. *Left-right structure*

块

kuài (¥1.00)

   b. *Left-center-right structure*

谢

xiè (thank)

3. a. *Top-bottom structure*

员

yuán (personnel, staff, member of)

   b. *Top-center-bottom structure*

曼

màn (graceful)

4. *Outer-inner structure*

圆

yuán (¥1.00)

CHINESE RADICALS

In Chinese dictionaries, the characters are arranged and indexed according to a list of radicals (bùshǒu 部首). "Bù" means "components" or "parts" and "shǒu" means "the head." A radical is the head part of the components from which a character is identified. Some characters have as many as eight components, but only one of the components is the radical. Often the radical is a component that is associated with the meaning of the character. If a character has two components, one usually is a pronunciation symbol and the other is an ideograph symbol that is associated with the meaning of the character and is the radical. For example:

Character	Radical for meaning	Component for pronunciation
们 (mén, plural for people)	亻 "human" radical	门 (mén)
妈 (mā, mother)	女 "woman" radical	马 (mǎ)
圆 (yuán, ¥1.00)	囗 "enclosure" radical	员 (yuán)

Some single-structure characters are arranged and indexed under a radical that is not related to meaning or sound, as in these examples:

Radical	Characters	
丿	九 (jiǔ, nine)	川 (chuān, river)
丨	书 (shū, book)	中 (zhōng, middle)

In 1983, the Chinese Character Reform Committee published 227 radicals that are officially used for indexing characters in Chinese dictionaries, such as the standard *Modern Chinese Dictionary* (Xiàndài Hànyǔ Cídiǎn 现代汉语词典). In order to find the meaning of an unknown character in a Chinese dictionary, you need to know the radical classification. Some radicals or Chinese characters are also used as components of other characters. For example:

女 nǚ:	妈 mā	她 tā	姐 jiě	妹 mèi
马 mǎ:	吗 ma	蚂 má	码 mǎ	骂 mà
中 zhōng:	钟 zhōng	忠 zhōng	仲 zhòng	种 zhòng

Learning radicals is a powerful aid in learning Chinese characters because many Chinese characters share the same radical or components. Characters that use the same radical are also often associated either in meaning or pronunciation. It is very helpful to learn radicals one by one. If you remember radicals and components, learning Chinese characters will become easier.

1. Identify the strokes used in the following Chinese characters.

三　小　六　丁　勺
九　八　人　女　水
山　买　又　冲　永

2. Identify the correct stroke order for each of the following characters.

毛　六　二　丁
什　人　八　儿
十　千　万　寸
小　水　子　永
月　风　问　用
国　圆　目　四

3. Identify the structure of each of the following characters as single, left-right, top-bottom, or inner-outer.

四　九　他　零
你　是　圆　好
五　很　六　们
谢　慢　谁　喜

Stroke Practice

The basic rules of writing the strokes are: "from left to right" and "from top to bottom":

一 _____

丨 _____

丿 _____

乀 _____

、 _____

灬 _____

亅 _____

乚 _____

一 _____

乛 _____

弋 _____

乙 _____

⺄ _____

乚 _____

乚 _____

く _____

ノ _____

2 Numbers

第 二 课　数字

Dì èr kè　　　　　　*Shùzì*

In this lesson you will learn to read and write twelve Chinese numbers.

With these twelve characters, you will be able to read and write all the numbers from 1 to 9,999.

Twelve characters for numbers
Four radicals
Structure of the characters
Practice reading number character combinations
Matching characters with their Pinyin
Reading numbers in years and in telephone numbers
Practice identifying word divisions in Chinese sentences
Practice writing radicals and characters
Practice writing characters with Chinese word-processing software,
    using the Pinyin input method
Numbers and the Creation of the Universe
Numbers That Are Also Radicals

NEW CHARACTERS

一	二	三	四	五	六
yī	èr	sān	sì	wǔ	liù
one	*two*	*three*	*four*	*five*	*six*

七	八	九	十	百	千
qī	bā	jiǔ	shí	bǎi	qiān
seven	*eight*	*nine*	*ten*	*hundred*	*thousand*

Suzhou garden

Understanding Chinese radicals can help you learn to read, write, and remember characters more quickly. Learn these four radicals:

口 enclosure	四 sì	圆 yuán	国 guó
儿 child	儿 ér	元 yuán	兑 duì
白 white	白 bái	百 bǎi	的 de
冖 cover	六 liù	京 jīng	旁 páng

STRUCTURE OF THE CHARACTERS

Chinese characters usually contain several components. In each character, one of the components is the radical and is the basis for indexing the character in a Chinese dictionary.

Learn the radicals and components of the following twelve Chinese characters. Remember that because the components of a character often are used in other characters and sometimes are themselves an individual character, when you learn one character you actually are learning two or more characters at the same time. In the chart, the components that are radicals are labeled with an "R," and the components that are independent characters are shown with their Pinyin pronunciation and their meaning in parentheses.

一	一 yī (one R)
二	二 èr (two R)
三	一 yī (one R) + 一 + 一
四	四 sì (four R) = 口 (enclosure) + 儿 ér (child)
五	一 yī (one R) or 二 èr (two R)
六	冖 (cover R) + 八 bā (eight)
七	一 yī (one R) + 乚
八	八 bā (eight R)

九	ノ (diagonal R) + 乙 yǐ (second)
十	十 shí (ten R)
百	一 yī (one R) + 白 bái (white)
千	ノ (diagonal on the top R) + 十 shí (ten)

READING PRACTICE

1. Read the following words. These are compounds of two or more numbers. Try to guess the meaning of each compound before you look at the English translations given below.

一	一十, 十一
二	二十, 十二, 二十一, 二十二
三	十三, 三十, 三十一, 三十二
四	十四, 四十, 四十一, 四十二, 四十三
五	十五, 五十, 五十四, 五十三, 五十二, 五十一
六	十六, 六十, 六十一, 六十三, 六十二, 六十四, 六十五
七	十七, 七十七, 七十六, 七十五, 七十四, 七十三, 七十二
八	十八, 八十, 八十四, 八十五, 八十六, 八十七, 八十八
九	十九, 九十, 九十四, 九十五, 九十六, 九十七, 九十八
十	十一, 十二, 十三, 十四, 五十, 六十, 七十, 八十, 十九
百	一百, 四百, 五百, 六百, 七百, 八百二十, 九百三十一
千	三千, 六千四百, 七千五百二十, 八千一百, 九千九

English translations:

一 一十 10; 十一 11

二 二十 20; 十二 12; 二十一 21; 二十二 22

三 十三 13; 三十 30; 三十一 31; 三十二 32

四 十四 14; 四十 40; 四十一 41; 四十二 42; 四十三 43

五 十五 15; 五十 50; 五十四 54; 五十三 53; 五十二 52;
   五十一 51

六 十六 16; 六十 60; 六十一 61; 六十三 63; 六十二 62;
   六十四 64; 六十五 65

七 十七 17; 七十七 77; 七十六 76; 七十五 75; 七十四 74;
   七十三 73; 七十二 72

八 十八 18; 八十 80; 八十四 84; 八十五 85; 八十六 86;
   八十七 87; 八十八 88

九 十九 19; 九十 90; 九十四 94; 九十五 95; 九十六 96;
   九十七 97; 九十八 98

十 十一 11; 十二 12; 十三 13; 十四 14; 五十 50; 六十 60;
   七十 70; 八十 80; 十九 19

百 一百 100; 四百 400; 五百 500; 六百 600; 七百 700;
   八百二十 820; 九百三十一 931

千 三千 3,000; 六千四百 6,400; 七千五百二十 7,520;
   八千一百 8,100; 九千九 9,900

2. Match each character with its Pinyin.

四	qī	百	bā
九	qiān	六	bǎi
千	sì	五	liù
七	jiǔ	八	wǔ

3. Read the following years and telephone numbers.

一九四九，一九一一，一七七六，二₀₀四
六二七五·四九三一，三四五五·二九三₀
五七八二·六一四九，九九八七·二三五六

4. Because Chinese is printed without word divisions, the first step in reading Chinese is to recognize the words in a sentence. You need a lot of practice to do that. In the following paragraph, underline the characters you can recognize.

毕业的时候一个同学给我的留言是：经济一穷二白，性
格反三复四，爱好五颜六色，人生信条乱七八糟，以上
所写如果不是百分之百也八九不离十。

WRITING PRACTICE

Chinese Radical Practice

1. Practice writing these radicals, using the correct stroke order.

口 _____

口 _____

儿 _____

儿 _____

白 _____

白 _____

亠 _____

亠 _____

2. In the lines below, write in characters from anywhere in this book that contain the radical given at the start of the row.

口 _____

儿 _____

白 _____

亠 _____

Chinese Character Practice

Practice writing the following characters by first tracing their outlines, and then writing them on your own. Follow the correct stroke order given here.

一　一

二　一　二

三　一　二　三

四　丨　冂　冃　四　四

五　一　丅　圷　五

六　丶　亠　六　六

七　一　七

八　丿　八

九　丿　九

十　一　十

百 一 一 一 万 百 百

千 ´ 一 千

Writing Characters with Chinese Software

Write the following in Chinese characters using the Pinyin input method of your Chinese word-processing program. Alternatively, if you do not have access to a Chinese word-processing program, write out in handwriting the Pinyin with tones and the characters for each of these. The individual characters used in each of the following have been introduced in this lesson or a prior lesson.

1. 10, 9, 8, 7, 6, 5, 4, 3, 2, 1

2. 626-625-9941   212-914-7780   310-759-9534   814-802-9092
   609-280-6636   718-607-4133   206-424-0794   302-231-7096
   503-816-3397   202-919-6155   404-225-5525   415-808-7144
   512-915-4099

3. 1987   2004   1776   1949   1911
   1997   2000   1856   1623

Numbers and the Creation of the Universe

In Chinese culture, numbers are related to the creation of the universe. The beginning of the universe is indicated by yī. Heaven and earth and the division of yin and yang is represented by èr. Heaven, humans, and earth are represented by sān. The division of yin into four is represented by sì. The five elements occurring from yin and yang intersecting between heaven and earth are indicated by wǔ. Yin starting to change is associated with liù. Yang situating in the middle is represented by qī. Yin and yang departing from each other is represented by bā. Yang starting its circuitous change is indicated by jiǔ. And shí is the completion of all numbers and the center of four directions.

Numbers That Are Also Radicals

The following five numbers are radicals and so can be found as components of other Chinese characters:

一 one	一 yī	三 sān	五 wǔ	七 qī
二 two	二 èr	五 wǔ	元 yuán	井 jǐng
四 four	四 sì	罗 luó	罪 zuì	罚 fá
八 eight	八 bā	六 liù	共 gòng	公 gōng
十 ten	十 shí	千 qiān	卖 mài	协 xié

3 Money (1)
第 三 课　钱 (一)

Dì sān kè　　　　*Qián*

In this lesson you will learn to read and write twelve Chinese characters related to money.

With these twelve characters, you will be able to recognize Chinese currency, and to read prices at a market and exchange rates in a bank.

Twelve characters related to money
Five radicals
Structure of the characters
Practice reading character combinations
Matching characters with their Pinyin
Practice identifying word divisions in Chinese sentences
Practice writing radicals and characters
Practice writing characters with Chinese word-processing software,
   using the Pinyin input method

NEW CHARACTERS

元 yuán	¥1.00 (the basic unit of money), dollar
圆 yuán	¥1.00 (formal written form of 元 yuán), dollar
块 kuài	¥1.00 (colloquial form of 元 yuán), dollar; (measure word for things in chunks or solid pieces); chunk
毛 máo	¥0.10; a surname
角 jiǎo	¥0.10; corner, horn

分 fēn	¥0.01, cent, minute
人 rén	person, human
民 mín	people, citizen
币 bì	currency, money, coin
钱 qián	money, cash
外 wài	foreign country, the outside; external
两 liǎng	two; a few

LEARNING RADICALS

Learn these five radicals:

土 **earth**	土 tǔ	块 kuài	在 zài	坐 zuò
刀 ⺈ * **knife**	刀 dāo	分 fēn	奂 huàn	角 jiǎo
钅 **metal**	钱 qián	银 yín	钞 chāo	钟 zhōng
夕 **sunset**	夕 xí	外 wài	多 duō	名 míng

* When the "knife" radical comes at the top of a character it has a shortened form.

STRUCTURE OF THE CHARACTERS

Learn the radicals (R) and components of these twelve Chinese characters:

元　二 èr (two R) + 儿 ér (son)

圆　囗 (enclosure R) + 员 yuán (personnel, member)　员 = 口 kǒu (mouth) +
　　　　　　　　　　　　　　　　　　　　　　　　　　　　　　　　貝 bèi (cowry)

块　土 tǔ (earth R) + 夬 guài (one of the Sixty-four Diagrams)

毛　毛 máo (hair R)

角　角 jiǎo (horn R) = 𠂊 (knife) + 用 yòng (to use)

分　八 bā (eight R) + 刀 dāo (knife)

人　人 rén (person R)

民　乙 yǐ (second R)

币　丿 (diagonal on the top R) + 巾 jīn (towel, scarf, kerchief)

钱　钅 (metal R) + 戋 jiān (tiny)

外　夕 xī (sunset R) + 卜 bǔ (divination)

两　一 yī (one R) + 冂 + 从 cóng (follow)

READING PRACTICE

1. Read the following words. These are compounds that combine a number with other characters. Try to guess the meaning of each compound before you look at the English translations given below.

元　一元, 五元, 十, 二十元, 三十六元

圆　一圆, 五圆, 十圆, 二十圆

块　七块, 十一块五, 九十九块八

毛　四毛, 八毛五, 十块三毛

角　三角, 五角四分, 九块七毛六分

分　一分, 百分, 千分

人　人人, 一百人

民	人民
币	人民币, 分币, 钱币, 一千元人民币
钱	一块钱, 四分钱, 六毛钱
外	外币, 外人
两	两百, 两千, 两块, 两圆, 两角, 两分

English translations:

元	一元 ¥1; 五元 ¥5; 十元 ¥10; 二十元 ¥20; 三十六元 ¥36
圆	一圆 ¥1; 五圆 ¥5; 十圆 ¥10; 二十圆 ¥20
块	七块 ¥7; 十一块五 ¥11.50; 九十九块八 ¥99.80
毛	四毛 ¥0.40; 八毛五 ¥0.85; 十块三毛 ¥10.30
角	三角 ¥0.30; 五角四分 ¥0.54; 九块七毛六分 ¥9.76
分	一分 ¥0.01; 百分 percent, 100 percent
人	人人 everyone; 一百人 100 people
民	人民 the people
币	人民币 People's currency; 分币 ¥0.01, cent; 钱币 coin; 一千元人民币 ¥1,000 RMB
钱	一块钱 ¥1; 四分钱 ¥0.04; 六毛钱 ¥0.60
外	外币 foreign currency; 外人 outsider
两	两百 200; 两千 2,000; 两块 ¥2; 两圆 ¥2; 两角 ¥0.20; 两分 ¥0.02

2. Match each character with its Pinyin.

圆	rén	币	wài
人	fēn	毛	yuán
角	mín	块	bì
分	yuán	外	kuài
民	jiǎo	元	máo

3. Underline the characters you can recognize in the following paragraph.

中国人民银行发行第三批第五套人民币。

中国人民银行决定从二零零一年九月一日起在全国发行
第三批第五套人民币，新的人民币有五十元，十元和两
角的纸币,二分的分币。

WRITING PRACTICE

Chinese Radical Practice

1. Practice writing these radicals, using the correct stroke order:

土 _____

土 _____

刀 _____

刀 _____

角 _____

角 _____

角 _____

角 _____

钅 _____

钅 _____

夕 _____

夕 _____

2. In the lines below, write in characters from anywhere in this book that contain the radical given at the start of the row.

土 _____

刀 _____

宀 _____

角 _____

钅 _____

夕 _____

3. What are the radicals in the characters below?

五 _____ 元 _____ 分 _____

四 _____ 千 _____ 块 _____

圆 _____ 百 _____ 六 _____

钱 _____ 外 _____ 角 _____

Bank of China deposit book

Chinese Character Practice

Practice writing the following characters by first tracing their outlines, and then writing them on your own. Follow the correct stroke order given here.

Writing Characters with Chinese Software

Write the following in Chinese characters using the Pinyin input method of your Chinese word-processing program. Alternatively, if you do not have access to a Chinese word-processing program, write out in handwriting the Pinyin with tones and the characters for each of these. The individual characters used in each of the following have been introduced in this lesson or a prior lesson.

1. ¥30.56   2. ¥2.42   3. ¥117.50   4. ¥1,988   5. money   6. people

7. foreign currency   8. one hundred people   9. circle

4 Money (2)

第四课　钱（二）

Dì sì kè　　　　*Qián*

In this lesson you will learn to read and write twelve more Chinese characters related to money.

These twelve Chinese characters, along with the characters from last lesson, will help you to read the names of banks, foreign currencies, and exchange rates in the bank.

- Twelve characters related to money
- Four radicals
- Structure of the characters
- Practice reading character combinations
- Reading signs and a listing of currency exchange rates
- Practice identifying word divisions in Chinese sentences
- Practice reading sentences
- Practice writing radicals and characters
- Practice writing characters with Chinese word-processing software, using the Pinyin input method

NEW CHARACTERS

中 zhōng	middle; China (short form of 中国 Zhōngguó)
国 guó	country
银 yín	silver, relating to money
行 háng/xíng	line, profession; to walk; OK
兑 duì	to exchange, to convert

换	to exchange, to trade, to change
huàn	
欧	Europe (short form of 欧洲 Ōuzhōu)
ōu	
美	beautiful; America (short form of 美国 Měiguó)
měi	
英	British (short form of 英国 Yīngguó)
yīng	
镑	pound
bàng	
港	port; Hong Kong (short form of 香港 Xiānggǎng)
gǎng	
台	stand; (short form of 台湾 Táiwān)
tái	

LEARNING RADICALS

Learn these four radicals:

彳	行	很	往	街
step	háng/xíng	hěn	wǎng/wàng	jiē
扌	拌	换	打	拨
hand	bàn	huàn	dǎ	bō
欠	欠	欧	次	欢
owe	qiàn	ōu	cì	huān
厶	台	去	叁	能
private	tái	qù	sān	néng

STRUCTURE OF THE CHARACTERS

Learn the radicals (R) and components of these twelve Chinese characters:

中　丨 (R)

国　口 (enclosure R) + 玉 yù (jade)　玉 = 王 wáng (king) + 丶

银　钅 (metal R) + 艮 gěn (blunt)

行　彳 (step R) + 亍 chù (surname)

兑　丷 (八 eight R) + 口 kǒu (mouth) + 儿 ér (son)

换　扌 (hand R) + 奂 huàn (numerous)

欧　欠 qiàn (owe R) + 区 qū (area)

美　羊 (羊 sheep R) + 大 dà (big)

英　艹 (grass R) + 央 yāng (center)

镑　钅 (metal R) + 旁 páng (side)

港　氵 (water R) + 巷 xiàng (alley)

　　巷 = 共 + 八 + 巳 sì (the sixth of the twelve Earthly Branches)

台　厶 (private R) + 口 kǒu (mouth)

READING PRACTICE

1. Read the following words. These are compounds that combine a character from this lesson with other characters you have learned before. Don't memorize the meaning of those words. Try to analyze the meaning of each compound when you read, then look at the English translations given below to check if you get the correct meaning from the reading.

中　中国, 中国人, 中国银行, 中国人民, 中外

国　国人, 国民, 国外, 外国, 外国人

银　银行, 银币, 银圆

行　人民银行, 中国银行, 外行, 一行, 行, 行人

兑　兑换, 外币兑换, 人民币兑换外币

换　换外币, 换人民币, 换一百块, 换人

Lesson 4: Money (2)

欧	欧元，欧圆，两千块欧元，欧美，中欧
美	美元，美圆，美国，美国人，美国人民，中美
英	英国，英国人，中英，英美，英两
镑	英镑
港	港币，兑换港币，港人，港英，一百块港币
台	台币，港台，一台

English translations:

中	中国 China; 中国人 Chinese; 中国人民 people of China; 中外 China and foreign
国	国人 fellow countrymen; 国民 national; 国外 abroad; 外国 foreign country; 外国人 foreigner
银	银行 bank; 银币 silver coin; 银圆 silver yuan
行	人民银行 People's Bank; 中国银行 Bank of China; 外行 laymen; 一行 one line; 行 (xíng) OK; 行人 pedestrian
兑	兑换 exchange; 外币兑换 foreign currency exchange; 人民币兑换外币 RMB exchange for foreign currency

500 Hong Kong dollars

换	换外币 to exchange foreign currency; 换人民币 to exchange RMB; 换一百块 to exchange 100 yuan; 换人 substitution of players
欧	欧元 Euro; 欧圆 Euro; 两千块欧元 2,000 Euros; 欧美 Europe and America; 中欧 Central Europe
美	美元 dollar; 美圆 dollar; 美国 United States; 美国人 American; 美国人民 people of America; 中美 China and America
英	英国 Britain, England, the United Kingdom; 英国人 Englishmen; 中英 China and Britain; 英美 Britain and United States; 英两 ounce
镑	英镑 pound
港	港币 HK$; 兑换港币 exchange HK$; 港人 Hong Kong people; 港英 Hong Kong and Britain; 一百块港币 HK$100
台	台币 Taiwan currency; 港台 Hong Kong and Taiwan; 一台 (measure word)

2. Read the following signs.

人民银行

外币兑换

中国银行

3. Point out the currencies you know in this exchange rate table.

兑换率 (lǜ, rate)	
外币	**人民币**
美元 100	826.42
英镑 100	1,515.53
欧元 100	994.14
台币 100	23.75
港币 100	105.98

4. Underline the characters you recognize in the following paragraph.

外币兑换

收兑币种

英镑，美元，瑞士法郎，德国马克，法国法郎，新加坡元，荷兰盾，瑞典克郎，丹麦克郎，挪威克郎，奥地利先令，比利时法郎，意大利里拉，日圆，加拿大元，澳大利亚元，芬兰马克，菲律宾比索，泰国币十九种外国货币及港币，新台币，澳元共二十三种货币，另外，以欧元和西班牙比塞塔为面值的支票也可兑换人民币。

5. Read the following sentences.

a. 人民币换美圆。

b. 港币换英镑。

c. 英国人换港币。

d. 台币换欧元。

e. 外国人换人民币。

f. 中国人换外币。

WRITING PRACTICE

Chinese Radical Practice

1. Practice writing these radicals, using the correct stroke order.

彳 _____

彳 _____

扌 _____

扌 _____

Success with Chinese: Reading & Writing

欠 _____

欠 _____

厶 _____

厶 _____

2. In the lines below, write in characters from anywhere in this book that contain the radical given at the start of the row.

彳 _____

扌 _____

欠 _____

厶 _____

Chinese Character Practice

Practice writing the following characters by first tracing their outlines, and then writing them on your own. Follow the correct stroke order given here.

中	丶	冖	口	中									

国	丨	冂	冂	冃	用	囯	国	国					

银	丿	⺊	⺊	⻐	钅	钅	钌	钌	钼	银	银		

行	丿	彳	彳	彳	行	行							

兑	丶	⺍	⺍	兑	台	尸	兑						

换	一	十	扌	扌	扩	护	护	护	换	换			

欧	一	丆	乂	区	区	欧	欧	欧					

Writing Characters with Chinese Software

Write the following in Chinese characters using the Pinyin input method of your Chinese word-processing program. Alternatively, if you do not have access to a Chinese word-processing program, write out in handwriting the Pinyin with tones and the characters for each of these. The individual characters used in each of the following have been introduced in this lesson or a prior lesson.

1. People's currency
2. Euro
3. exchange HK$ into American dollars
4. exchange American dollars into Taiwan currency
5. Chinese people

6. Britain and United States
7. foreign currency exchange
8. China and foreign countries
9. China and United States
10. exchange US$100 to English pounds

5 Foods

第五课　食物

Dì wǔ kè　Shíwù

In this lesson you will begin to learn how to read restaurant menus.

In each of Lessons Five through Nine you will learn twelve Chinese characters that appear in almost every Chinese menu. When you see these characters in the names of dishes you will learn important general information such as whether the dish has rice or noodles, fish or chicken, or is a dish or a soup. You use these words to analyze the contents of a dish in a menu.

Twelve basic characters that appear in almost every Chinese menu
Four radicals
Structure of the characters
Practice reading the names of dishes on menus
Read a sample menu
Practice identifying word divisions in Chinese sentences
Practice writing radicals and characters
Practice writing characters with Chinese word-processing software, using the Pinyin input method

NEW CHARACTERS

菜 cài	dish; vegetable
汤 tāng	soup
面 miàn	noodle, flour
米 mǐ	uncooked rice; meter
饭 fàn	meal; cooked rice

饼 bǐng	fried bread
馒(头) mán(tou)	steamed bread, steamed bun
头 tóu	head, chief, end
蛋 dàn	eggs
肉 ròu	meat
鸡 jī	chicken
鱼 yú	fish

At a market

Success with Chinese: Reading & Writing

Learn these four radicals:

⻟	饭	馆	馒	饼	饺	饮
food	fàn	guǎn	mán	bǐng	jiǎo	yǐn
艹	菜	茶	蒸	葱	茄	英
grass	cài	chá	zhēng	cōng	qié	yīng
氵	汤	清	滑	溜		
water	tāng	qīng	huá	liū		
虫	虫	虾	蛋			
insect	cóng	xiā	dàn			

STRUCTURE OF THE CHARACTERS

Learn the radicals (R) and components of these twelve Chinese characters:

菜	艹 (grass R) + 采 cǎi (pick); 采 = ⺥ + 木 mù (wood)
汤	氵 (water R)
面	一 yī (R) → 丆 + 囬 huí (return)
米	米 (rice R) = ⅋ + 木 mù
饭	⻟ (food R) + 反 fǎn (reverse); 反 = 厂 + 又 yòu (again)
饼	⻟ (food R) + 并 bìng (combine)
馒	⻟ (food R) + 曼 màn (graceful); 曼 = 日 rì (sun) + 罒 sì (four) + 又 yòu (again)
头	、 + 大 dà (big R)
蛋	疋 pǐ (measure word R) + 虫 chóng (insect R)
肉	冂 (R) + 仌 (two 人 rén: person)
鸡	又 yòu (R) + 鸟 niǎo (bird R)
鱼	鱼 yú (fish R) = ⺈ (knife) + 田 tián (field) + 一 yī (one)

1. Read the following words. These are compounds that combine a character from this lesson with other characters you have learned before. Don't memorize the meaning of those words. Try to analyze the meaning of each compound when you read, then look at the English translations given below to check if you get the correct meaning from the reading.

菜	菜汤, 肉菜
汤	汤面, 鸡蛋汤, 肉汤, 鸡汤, 鱼汤, 汤圆
面	面汤, 肉面, 鸡蛋面
米	米饭, 米面, 一百米
饭	饭菜, 中国饭, 英国饭, 美国饭
饼	肉饼, 菜饼
馒	馒头
头	头人, 人头, 一头
蛋	蛋汤, 蛋饼, 鸡蛋
肉	肉菜, 肉饼, 肉面
鸡	鸡肉, 鸡肉面, 鸡蛋饼, 鸡头
鱼	鱼头, 鱼肉, 面鱼

English translations:

菜	菜汤 vegetable soup; 肉菜 meat dish
汤	汤面 noodles in soup; 鸡蛋汤 egg-drop soup; 肉汤 meat soup; 鸡汤 chicken soup; 鱼汤 fish soup; 汤圆 dumpling (round shape, made of sticky rice with sweet stuffing)
面	肉面 noodles with meat; 鸡蛋面 noodles with crumbled eggs
米	米饭 cooked rice; 米面 rice and flour; 一百米 hundred meters
饭	饭菜 rice and dishes; 中国饭 Chinese food; 英国饭 English food; 美国饭 American food
饼	肉饼 fried bread with meat filling; 菜饼 fried bread with vegetable filling
馒	馒头 steamed bread

头	头人 headman; 人头 human head; 一头 (measure word)
蛋	蛋汤 egg-drop soup; 蛋饼 egg pancake; 鸡蛋 chicken eggs
肉	肉菜 meat dish; 肉面 noodles with meat; 肉饼 fried-bread with meat filling
鸡	鸡肉 chicken meat; 鸡肉面 noodles with chicken meat;
	鸡蛋饼 egg pancake; 鸡头 chicken head
鱼	鱼头 fish head; 鱼肉 fish meat; 面鱼 fish-shaped noodles

2. Read this menu and look for the chicken, fish, and meat dishes. How many chicken dishes are listed? How many fish dishes? How many meat dishes?

MENU

青菜

炒素菜	¥6.00
炒鸡蛋	¥10.00

肉菜

辣子鸡丁	¥16.00
炒肉片	¥15.00
红烧鱼	¥30.00

汤

素菜汤	¥6.00
鸡蛋汤	¥8.00
鱼汤	¥10.00

主食 (zhǔshí, staple food)

米饭	¥1.00
馒头	¥0.50/个
牛肉饼	¥2.00/个
面条	¥8.00
汤面	¥10.00

3. Underline the characters you can recognize in the following paragraph.

上海菜又叫本帮菜，主要取用本地鱼虾蔬菜，上海本帮
名菜中，清淡素雅的首推夏秋季节的糟食，如糟鸡，糟
毛豆，糟茭白，滑炒虾仁，冰糖甲鱼，芙蓉鸡片，糯米
丸子等。上海的汤包，八宝饭，小馒头也很著名。

WRITING PRACTICE

Chinese Radical Practice

1. Practice writing these radicals, using the correct stroke order.

飠 _____

飠 _____

艹 _____

艹 _____

氵 _____

氵 _____

虫 _____

虫 _____

2. In the lines below, write in characters from anywhere in this book that contain the radical given at the start of the row.

飠 _____

艹 _____

氵 _____

虫 _____

Chinese Character Practice

Practice writing the following characters by first tracing their outlines, and then writing them on your own. Follow the correct stroke order given here.

| 菜 | 一 | 十 | 艹 | 艹 | 艺 | 苹 | 苹 | 莖 | 苹 | 菜 | | | | | | |

| 汤 | 丶 | 冫 | 氵 | 氵 | 沔 | 汤 | 汤 | | | | | | | | |

| 面 | 一 | 丆 | 广 | 而 | 而 | 而 | 而 | 面 | 面 | | | | | | |

| 饼 | 丿 | 𠂊 | 饣 | 饣 | 饣 | 饣 | 饼 | 饼 | 饼 | | | | | | |

| 米 | 丶 | 丷 | 丷 | 半 | 米 | 米 | | | | | | | | | |

| 饭 | 丿 | 𠂊 | 饣 | 饣 | 饣 | 饭 | 饭 | | | | | | | | |

| 馒 | 丿 | 𠂊 | 饣 | 饣 | 饣 | 饣 | 馒 | 馒 | 馒 | 馒 | 馒 | 馒 | | | |

| 头 | 丶 | ゛ | 二 | 头 | 头 | | | | | | | | | | |

| 蛋 | 一 | 𠃌 | 乛 | 乛 | 乛 | 疋 | 疋 | 蛋 | 蛋 | 蛋 | 蛋 | | | | |

| 肉 | 丨 | 冂 | 冈 | 内 | 肉 | 肉 | | | | | | | | | |

| 鸡 | 刁 | 又 | 又 | 𡿨 | 𡿨 | 鸡 | 鸡 | | | | | | | | |

| 鱼 | 丿 | 𠂊 | 𠂊 | 各 | 鱼 | 鱼 | 鱼 | 鱼 | | | | | | | |

Writing Characters with Chinese Software

Write the following in Chinese characters using the Pinyin input method of your Chinese word-processing program. Alternatively, if you do not have access to a Chinese word-processing program, write out in handwriting the Pinyin with tones and the characters for each of these. The individual characters used in each of the following have been introduced in this lesson or a prior lesson.

1. Egg-drop soup   2. Noodles in soup   3. Rice, steamed bread   4. Vegetable dish, meat dish

6

Tastes & Cooking Methods

第六课　味道和烹调

Dì liù kè　　*Wèidào hé pēngtiáo*

In this lesson you will learn twelve Chinese characters for the taste of food and the methods of cooking.

They are basic terms that appear in almost every Chinese menu. When you find these characters in the name of a dish, you will know what the taste of that dish is and how it is cooked.

- Twelve basic characters that appear in almost every Chinese menu
- Four radicals
- Structure of the characters
- Practice reading the names of dishes
- Practice reading sample menus
- Practice identifying word divisions in Chinese sentences
- Practice writing radicals and characters
- Practice writing characters with Chinese word-processing software, using the Pinyin input method

NEW CHARACTERS

糖 táng	sugar, sweets, candy
辣 là	spicy, hot
醋 cù	vinegar
酸 suān	sour

酱 jiàng	soy bean sauce, sauce, jam, cooked in soy sauce
油 yóu	oil, grease
炒 chǎo	to stir-fry
炸 zhá/zhà	to fry in oil, to deep fry
爆 bào	to quick fry; explode
烧 shāo	to stew, to cook, to roast
拌 bàn	to stir and mix (with sauce)
蒸 zhēng	to steam

LEARNING RADICALS

Learn these four radicals:

火 fire	烧 shāo	炒 chǎo	爆 bào	炸 zhá
灬 four dots	蒸 zhēng			
米 rice	料 liào	糖 táng		
酉 yǒu (the tenth of the twelve Earthly Branches)			酸 suān	酱 jiàng	醋 cù

STRUCTURE OF THE CHARACTERS

Learn the radicals (R) and components of these twelve Chinese characters:

糖	米 mǐ (rice R) + 唐 Táng (surname);
	唐 = 广 guǎng (broad) + 肀 (hand R) + 口 kǒu (mouth)
辣	辛 xīn (hot R) + 束 shù (to tie)
醋	酉 yǒu (the tenth of the twelve Earthly Branches R) + 昔 xī (the past);
	昔 = 龷 + 日 rì (sun)
酸	酉 yǒu (R) + 厶 (private) + 八 bā (eight) + 夂 (script) [reversed wén 文]
酱	酉 yǒu (R) + 丬 + 夕 xí (sunset)
炒	火 huǒ (fire R) + 少 shǎo (little)
炸	火 huǒ (fire R) + 乍 zhà (first)
爆	火 huǒ (fire R) + 暴 bào (violent);
	暴 = 日 rì (sun) + 共 gòng (altogether) + 氺
烧	火 huǒ (fire R) + 尧 Yáo (surname)
拌	扌 (hand R) + 半 bàn (half)
蒸	艹 (grass R) + 丞 chéng (assist) + 灬 [four dots R]

READING PRACTICE

1. Read the following words. These are compounds that combine a character from this lesson with other characters you have learned before. Don't memorize the meaning of those words. Try to analyze the meaning of each compound when you read, then look at the English translations given below to check if you get the correct meaning from the reading.

糖	糖醋, 糖醋肉, 糖醋鱼
辣	辣子, 辣子肉, 辣子鸡, 辣面
醋	醋鱼
酸	酸辣, 酸辣汤, 酸辣鱼
酱	酱油, 酱菜, 辣酱, 酱鸡

油　油饼, 油菜, 菜油
炒　炒饭, 炒菜, 炒面, 炒鸡蛋, 炒饼
炸　炸鸡, 炸鱼, 炸鸡蛋, 油炸, 炸酱面
爆　爆炒, 酱爆, 油爆
烧　烧鸡, 烧鸡块, 烧肉, 烧饼, 烧饭
拌　拌菜, 拌面
蒸　蒸肉, 蒸鱼, 蒸饼

English translations:

糖　糖醋 sweet-and-sour; 糖醋肉 sweet-and-sour pork;
　　糖醋鱼 sweet-and-sour fish

辣　辣子 chili; 辣子肉 spicy pork; 辣子鸡 spicy chicken;
　　辣面 spicy noodles

醋　醋鱼 fish cooked in vinegar sauce

酸　酸辣 hot-and-sour; 酸辣汤 hot-and-sour soup;
　　酸辣鱼 hot-and-sour fish

酱　酱油 soy sauce; 酱菜 pickle; 辣酱 thick chili sauce;
　　酱鸡 chicken cooked in soy sauce

油　油饼 deep-fried flat bread; 油菜 rapé; 菜油 vegetable oil

炒　炒饭 fried rice; 炒菜 stir-fried dish; 炒面 stir-fried noodles;
　　炒鸡蛋 scrambled eggs; 炒饼 stir-fried strips of fried bread

炸　炸鸡 fried chicken; 炸鱼 fried fish; 炸鸡蛋 eggs sunny-side up;
　　油炸 to deep fry; 炸酱面 noodles with soy bean sauce

爆　爆炒 to quick-fry; 酱爆 quick-fried in bean paste; 油爆 quick-fried in oil

烧　烧鸡 roasted chicken; 烧鸡块 stewed chicken chunks;
　　烧肉 stewed pork; 烧饼 sesame seed cake; 烧饭 to cook a meal

拌　拌菜 mixed vegetables with sauce; 拌面 noodles mixed with sauce

蒸　蒸肉 steamed pork; 蒸鱼 steamed fish; 蒸饼 steamed flat bread

2. Read this sign.

早点 (zǎodiǎn, breakfast)	
烧饼	¥2.00
油饼	¥5.00
蛋饼	¥5.00
炸鸡蛋	¥3.00
汤面	¥8.00

3. Read this menu and look for the chicken, fish, and meat dishes. How many chicken dishes are listed? How many fish dishes? How many meat dishes?

MENU	
素菜	
拌素菜	¥6.50
炒油菜	¥8.00
炒鸡蛋	¥10.00
肉菜	
辣子鸡	¥18.00
油菜炒肉	¥15.00
酱爆肉	¥18.00
糖醋鱼	¥25.00
烧鱼块	¥22.00
蒸鱼	¥25.00
烧鸡	¥38.00
汤	
素菜汤	¥8.00
鸡蛋汤	¥8.00
酸辣汤	¥10.00

(continued on next page)

主食 (zhǔshí, staple food)	
米饭	¥2.00
馒头	¥1.00/个
炒面	¥12.00/个
鸡蛋炒饭	¥12.00
炸酱面	¥10.00

4. Underline the characters you can recognize in the following paragraph.

北京菜的烹调方法全面众多，以爆，烤，涮，炝，溜，炸，烧，炒，扒，煨，焖，酱，拔丝，白煮，拌等技法见长。北京菜的"爆"法，变化多样，具体可分为油爆，酱爆，葱爆，水爆，汤爆等。口味讲究酥脆鲜嫩，清鲜爽口，保持原味，并且要求做到色，香，味，形，器五方面俱佳。

5. Read these names of Chinese dishes.

a. 素菜炒饼

b. 酸菜烧肉

c. 鸡肉汤面

d. 糖醋肉

e. 酱爆鸡

f. 酸辣鱼

WRITING PRACTICE

Chinese Radical Practice

1. Practice writing these radicals, using the correct stroke order.

火 _____

火 _____

灬 _____

灬 _____

米 _____

米 _____

酉 _____

酉 _____

2. In the lines below, write in characters from anywhere in this book that contain the radical given at the start of the row.

火 _____

灬 _____

米 _____

酉 _____

Chinese Character Practice

Practice writing the following characters by first tracing their outlines, and then writing them on your own. Follow the correct stroke order given here.

糖	丶	丷	亅	半	米	米	米	糖	糖	糖	糖	糖	糖	糖
辣	丶	二	三	玄	立	立	辛	辛	辛	辣	辣	辣		
子	㇇	了	子											
醋	一	厂	币	丙	丙	酉	酉	酉	酉	醋	醋	醋	醋	醋

Lesson 6: Tastes & Cooking Methods

Writing Characters with Chinese Software

Write the following in Chinese characters using the Pinyin input method of your Chinese word-processing program. Alternatively, if you do not have access to a Chinese word-processing program, write out in handwriting the Pinyin with tones and the characters for each of these. The individual characters used in each of the following have been introduced in this lesson or a prior lesson.

1. stir-fried vegetables
2. scrambled eggs
3. spicy chicken noodles
4. sweet-and-sour soup

5. fried rice with eggs
6. pickles
7. steamed fish

8. quick-fried pork
9. fried fish
10. mixed vegetables with sauce

7 Cutting Methods & Kinds of Food

第七课　形状和食物

Dì qī kè　Xíngzhuàng hé shíwù

In this lesson you will continue to learn how to read restaurant menus.

Fourteen characters that appear in the names of dishes. You use these words to analyze the contents of a dish in a menu.

Four radicals

Structure of the characters

Practice reading character combinations that are the names of dishes on menus

Practice identifying word divisions in Chinese sentences

Translate Chinese phrases into English

Read sample menus

Practice writing radicals and characters

Practice writing characters with Chinese word-processing software, using the Pinyin input method

NEW CHARACTERS

丝 sī	threadlike, silk
丁 dīng	cube, diced piece
片 piàn	slice, thin piece (measure word)
条 tiáo	strip; measure word for long, narrow things
豆 dòu	beans, peas

腐 fŭ	bean curd; to decay
饺（子） jiǎo	dumpling with vegetable &/or meat stuffing
牛 niú	cow
鸭 yā	duck
虾 xiā	shrimp
素 sù	plain, vegetable
葱 cōng	green onion
瓜 guā	melon, gourd
椒 jiāo	hot pepper plant

LEARNING RADICALS

Learn these four radicals:

纟 **silk**	丝 sī	红 hóng	绿 lù	给 gěi		
广 **broad**	广 guǎng	腐 fŭ	唐 táng	店 diàn	床 chuáng	麻 má
鸟 **bird**	鸟 niǎo	鸭 yā	鸡 jī	鹅 é	鸽 gē	
心 **heart**	葱 cōng	您 nín	怎 zěn	息 xī		

STRUCTURE OF THE CHARACTERS

Learn the radicals (R) and components of these twelve Chinese characters:

丝	纟 (silk R) + 纟
丁	一 yī (one R) + 亅
片	片 piàn (slice R)
条	夂 (R) + 木 mù (wood)
豆	豆 dòu (beans R) = 一 + 口 + 丷 + 一
腐	广 guǎng (broad R) + 肉 ròu (meat R) + 付 fù (pay);
	付 = 亻 + 寸 cùn (1/10 meter)
饺	饣 (food R) + 交 jiāo (hand over)
牛	牛 niú (cow R)
鸭	鸟 niǎo (bird R) + 甲 jiǎ (the first of the Heavenly Stems)
虾	虫 chóng (insect R) + 下 xià (under)
素	丰 + 糸 sī (silk R)
葱	艹 (grass R + 匆 cōng (hurriedly) + 心 xīn (heart)
瓜	瓜 guā (melon R)
椒	木 mù (wood R) + 叔 shū (uncle);
	叔 = 上 shàng (above) + 小 xiǎo (little) + 又 yòu (again)

READING PRACTICE

1. Read the following words. These are compounds that combine a character from this lesson with other characters you have learned before. Don't memorize the meaning of those words. Try to analyze the meaning of each compound when you read, then look at the English translations given below to check if you get the correct meaning from the reading.

丝	肉丝, 炒肉丝, 炒鸡丝, 拌三丝, 一丝
丁	鸡丁, 肉丁, 炒三丁, 炒辣子鸡丁
片	肉片, 炒肉片, 烧鱼片, 爆两片, 一片肉

条　面条, 油条, 一条鱼
豆　豆角, 豆子, 豆饼, 土豆, 豆油, 炸土豆片
腐　豆腐, 酱豆腐, 油豆腐
饺　饺子
牛　牛肉, 烧牛肉, 牛肉面
鸭　鸭子, 鸭肉, 烧鸭, 鸭蛋
虾　虾米, 虾酱, 虾子, 虾片, 炸虾, 油爆虾
素　素菜, 炒素菜, 素面
葱　葱爆, 葱油饼, 葱爆牛肉, 小葱, 葱头
瓜　丝瓜, 瓜子, 木瓜, 瓜分
椒　辣椒

English translations:

丝　肉丝 shredded pork; 炒肉丝 stir-fried shredded pork; 一丝 one shred; 炒鸡丝 stir-fried shredded chicken; 拌三丝 three mixed shredded things

丁　鸡丁 diced chicken; 肉丁 diced pork; 炒三丁 three stir-fried diced things; 炒辣子鸡丁 stir-fried spicy diced chicken

片　肉片 sliced meat; 炒肉片 stir-fried sliced meat; 烧鱼片 fish slices stewed after frying; 爆两片 two kinds of sliced meat quick-fried; 一片肉 one piece of meat

条　面条 noodles; 油条 deep-fried twisted dough sticks; 一条鱼 one fish

豆　豆角 green beans; 豆子 beans; 豆饼 soybean bread; 土豆 potato; 豆油 soybean oil; 炸土豆片 potato chips

腐　豆腐 tofu; 酱豆腐 fermented tofu; 油豆腐 fried tofu

饺　饺子 dumpling

牛　牛肉 beef; 烧牛肉 stewed beef; 牛肉面 beef noodles

鸭　鸭子 duck; 鸭肉 duck meat; 烧鸭 roasted duck; 鸭蛋 duck eggs

虾	虾米 dried shrimp; 虾酱 shrimp sauce; 虾子 shrimp roe;
	虾片 sliced shrimp; 炸虾 deep-fried shrimp; 油爆虾 quick-fried shrimp
素	素菜 vegetable dish; 炒素菜 stir-fried vegetables; 素面 vegetarian noodle
葱	葱爆 quick-fried with green onions; 葱爆牛肉 quick-fried sliced beef
	with green onions; 葱油饼 green onion fried bread; 小葱 green onion;
	葱头 onion
瓜	丝瓜 gourd; 瓜子 melon seeds; 木瓜 papaya; 瓜分 divided up
椒	辣椒 hot peppers

2. Read the following sign.

早点 (zǎodiǎn, breakfast)	
烧饼	¥2.00
油条	¥5.00
油饼	¥5.00
炸鸡蛋	¥3.00
饺子	¥12.00/斤 jīn
汤面	¥8.00

3. Underline the characters you can recognize in the following paragraph.

四川风味包括了成都，重庆，乐山，江津，自贡，合川
等地方菜的特色。素有"一菜一格，百菜百味"的佳
话，以麻，辣著称。川菜最大的特点在于调味。烹调多
用辣椒，胡椒，花椒，豆瓣酱和醋，糖来调味。
四川的风味小吃与面点同样出名。四川最负盛名的菜和
小吃有：干烧鲤鱼，鱼香猪肉丝，宫保鸡丁，生爆盐煎
肉，夫妻肺片，干煸牛肉丝，麻婆豆腐，羊肉火锅，担
担面，赖汤圆，龙抄手，叶儿粑等。

4. Translate the following into English.

a. 鸡丝拌辣面条

b. 肉片烧豆腐

c. 素炒豆角

d. 炸土豆片

e. 辣椒炒土豆丝

f. 木瓜，瓜子

A local restaurant

5. Read the menu and find the chicken, fish, and meat dishes. How many chicken dishes are listed? How many fish dishes? How many meat dishes?

MENU	
素菜	
拌三丝	¥6.50
炒丝瓜	¥6.00
素烧豆腐	¥8.00
炒鸡蛋	¥10.00
肉菜	
炒辣子鸡丁	¥14.00
酱爆肉丁	¥20.00
酸菜炒肉丝	¥15.00
爆两片	¥18.00
糖醋肉片	¥20.00
葱头炒肉片	¥16.00
蛋饺	¥18.00
酱豆腐肉	¥14.00
油爆虾	¥22.00
蒸鱼	¥35.00
烧鸭	¥48.00

汤	
素菜汤	¥5.00
鸡蛋汤	¥8.00
酸辣汤	¥10.00
鱼片汤	¥12.00

主食	
米饭	¥0.50
炸馒头	¥2.00/个
鸡蛋炒饭	¥6.00
饺子	¥14.00
面条	¥8.00
葱油饼	¥3.00/个

WRITING PRACTICE

Chinese Radical Practice

1. Practice writing these radicals, using the correct stroke order.

纟 _____

纟 _____

糸 _____

糸 _____

广 _____

广 _____

鸟 _____

鸟 _____

心 _____

心 _____

2. In the lines below, write in characters from anywhere in this book that contain the radical given at the start of the row.

纟 _____

糸 _____

广 _____

鸟 _____

心 _____

Chinese Character Practice

Practice writing the following characters by first tracing their outlines, and then writing them on your own. Follow the correct stroke order given here.

| 丝 | ⼂ | ⼁ | ⼃ | 丝 | 丝 | | | | | | | | | |

| 丁 | 一 | 丁 | | | | | | | | | | | | |

| 片 | 丿 | ⼁ | 广 | 产 | 片 | | | | | | | | | |

| 条 | 丿 | 夕 | 冬 | 冬 | 条 | 条 | 条 | | | | | | | |

| 豆 | 一 | ⼇ | 冖 | 口 | 戸 | 豆 | 豆 | | | | | | | |

| 腐 | 丶 | ⼇ | 广 | 广 | 广 | 庐 | 府 | 府 | 府 | 府 | 腐 | 腐 | 腐 | 腐 |

Writing Characters with Chinese Software

Write the following in Chinese characters using the Pinyin input method of your Chinese word-processing program. Alternatively, if you do not have access to a Chinese word-processing program, write out in handwriting the Pinyin with tones and the characters for each of these. The individual characters used in each of the following have been introduced in this lesson or a prior lesson.

1. stir-fried shredded chicken
2. stir-fried spicy diced tofu with pork
3. roasted duck
4. chili stir-fried shredded potato
5. noodles
6. vegetable dumpling
7. quick-fried sliced beef with green onions

8. stewed beef
9. deep-fried shrimp
10. stir-fried sliced shrimp
11. beef-noodle restaurant
12. restaurant
13. egg-drop soup
14. vegetarian restaurant

8 Drinks

第八课　饮料

Dì bā kè　　*Yǐnliào*

In this lesson you will learn basic terms related to drinks, for the purpose of reading restaurant menus.

Fourteen Chinese characters that are basic terms related to drinks
Four radicals
Structure of the characters
Practice reading character combinations related to drinks
Practice reading signs
Read a sample menu
Translate short sentences from Chinese into English
Practice identifying word divisions in Chinese sentences
Practice writing radicals and characters
Practice writing characters with Chinese word-processing software,
　　using the Pinyin input method

NEW CHARACTERS

饮 yǐn	a drink; to drink
料 liào	material, ingredient
水 shuǐ	water
茶 chá	tea
奶 nǎi	milk, breast
可 kě	co(la) (first character of 可乐 kělè); but; can, may

乐 lè	(co)la (second character of 可乐 kělè); happy*
啤 pí	beer
酒 jiǔ	liquor, wine
桔 jú	orange, tangerine
汁 zhī	juice
餐 cān	meal, to eat
馆 guǎn	shop, hall
不 bù	no, not

LEARNING RADICALS

Learn these four radicals:

口 **mouth**	口 kǒu	咖 kā	啡 fēi	可 kě	啤 pí	吃 chī	喝 hē
木 **wood**	条 tiáo	杯 bēi	桔 jú	橘 jú	果 guǒ	棍 gùn	
小 **small**	少 shǎo	尘 chén	尔 ěr	尝 cháng			
女 **female**	女 nǚ	奶 nǎi	好 hǎo	姐 jiě	要 yào	她 tā	婆 pó

*The compound name "Coca-Cola" is based on its sound in English.

STRUCTURE OF THE CHARACTERS

Learn the radicals (R) and components of these twelve Chinese characters:

饮	饣 (food R) + 欠 qiàn (owe)
料	米 mǐ (rice R) + 斗
水	水 shuǐ (water R)
茶	艹 (grass R) + 人 rén (person) + 木 mù (wood)
奶	女 nǔ (woman R) + 乃 nǎi (to be, therefore)
可	一 yī (one R) + 口 kǒu (mouth R) + 亅
乐	丿 (diagonal on the top R) + 小 xiǎo (little, small)
啤	口 kǒu (mouth R) + 卑 bēi (modest, low)
酒	氵 (water R) + 酉 yǒu (the tenth of the twelve Earthly Branches)
桔	木 mù (wood R) + 吉 jí (lucky) 吉 = 士 shì (scholar) + 口 kǒu (mouth)
汁	氵 (water R) + 十 shí (ten)
馆	饣 (food R) + 官 guān (officer) 官 = 宀 (roof R)
餐	食 shí (food-complex form R) + 夕 xī (sunset) + 又 yòu (again)
不	一 yī (one R)

READING PRACTICE

1. Read the following words. These are compounds that combine a character from this lesson with other characters you have learned before. Don't memorize the meaning of those words. Try to analyze the meaning of each compound when you read, then look at the English translations given below to check if you get the correct meaning from the reading.

饮	饮
料	饮料，料子，一料
水	饮水，兑水，水牛
茶	茶馆，茶水，饮茶，茶饭，茶钱
奶	奶茶，牛奶，奶奶
可	可可，可口，可饮水，可兑换

Lesson 8: Drinks   65

乐	可乐，可口可乐，快乐
啤	啤酒
酒	酒馆，饮酒，红酒，料酒，烧酒
桔	桔子，桔子水
汁	桔汁，桔子汁
餐	餐馆，中餐，美餐，一餐
馆	馆子，饭馆，素菜馆，牛肉面馆
不	不可，不饮，不炒，不蒸，不炸，不乐

English translations:

饮	饮 to drink
料	饮料 drinks, beverage; 料子 fabric; 一料 one prescription
水	饮水 drinking water; 兑水 add water, dilute; 水牛 buffalo
茶	茶馆 tea house; 茶水 tea water; 饮茶 dim sum; 茶饭 food and drink; 茶钱 tip
奶	奶茶 tea with milk; 牛奶 milk; 奶奶 grandma
可	可可 cocoa; 可口 tasty; 可饮水 drinking water; 可兑换 convertible
乐	可乐 cola (short form of 可口可乐 Kěkǒu Kělè); 可口可乐 Coca-Cola; 快乐 happy
啤	啤酒 beer
酒	酒馆 bar; 饮酒 drink (liquor); 料酒 cooking wine; 烧酒 spirit
桔	桔子 orange; 桔子水 orange juice
汁	桔汁 orange juice; 桔子汁 orange juice
餐	餐馆 restaurant; 中餐 Chinese food; 美餐 tasty food; 一餐 one meal
馆	馆子 restaurant; 饭馆 restaurant; 素菜馆 vegetarian restaurant; 牛肉面馆 beef noodle restaurant
不	不可 cannot; 不饮 not drink; 不炒 not stir-fry; 不蒸 not steam; 不炸 not deep fry; 不乐 not happy

2. Read the following signs.

人民饭馆

饮茶

可口可乐

快乐餐馆

素菜馆

牛肉面馆

3. Find as many drinks as you can on the following menu.

饮料	
茶	¥4.00
奶茶	¥8.00
桔汁	¥15.00
中国酒	¥30.00
外国酒	¥45.00
可乐	¥4.00
可可	¥10.00
水	¥3.00
啤酒	¥6.00

4. Translate the following sentences into English.

a. 中国酒辣不辣？

b. 少饮酒。

c. 快乐餐馆快乐不快乐？

d. 料酒不可饮。

e. 奶奶饮奶茶。

5. *Underline the characters you can recognize in the following paragraph.*

在中国的酒吧里你想喝什么都有。现在酒吧里最受欢迎的就是啤酒！红酒也渐渐流行起来。“长城干红”是红酒市场里最“抵饮”的品种了。如果你滴酒不沾的话，可以选择喝茶，雪碧，可乐，桔汁，鲜奶，或是咖啡。不过现在街头的咖啡厅也多了起来，在酒吧里就很少看到有人点咖啡了。在酒吧里不是酒类的饮料，价格可比外面高多了。

WRITING PRACTICE

Chinese Radical Practice

1. Practice writing these radicals, using the correct stroke order:

口 _____

口 _____

木 _____

木 _____

小 _____

小 _____

女 _____

女 _____

2. In the lines below, write in characters from anywhere in this book that contain the radical given at the start of the row.

口 _____

木 _____

小 _____

女 _____

Chinese Character Practice

Practice writing the following characters by first tracing their outlines, and then writing them on your own. Follow the correct stroke order given here.

饮	ノ	㇇	饣	饣	饮	饮	饮							
料	丶	丷	丷	半	米	米	米	米	料	料				
水	丿	刀	水	水										
茶	一	十	艹	艹	艾	苂	荟	茶	茶					
奶	𡿨	𠃌	女	奶	奶									
可	一	丆	丆	口	可									
乐	丿	𠂉	乐	乐	乐									
啤	丶	口	口	口'	叨	吼	咱	咱	啤	啤	啤			
酒	丶	氵	氵	汀	汀	沔	沔	酒	酒	酒				
桔	一	十	才	木	朴	村	枯	桔	桔	桔				

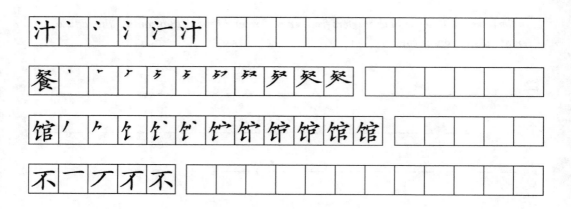

Writing Characters with Chinese Software

Write the following in Chinese characters using the Pinyin input method of your Chinese word-processing program. Alternatively, if you do not have access to a Chinese word-processing program, write out in handwriting the Pinyin with tones and the characters for each of these. The individual characters used in each of the following have been introduced in this lesson or a prior lesson.

1. fish braised in soy sauce
2. drinks
3. dim sum
4. black tea
5. American beer

6. bar
7. red wine
8. orange juice
9. Coca-Cola
10. drinking water

11. cafe
12. not happy
13. cannot
14. cooking wine

Success with Chinese: Reading & Writing

9 Reading Menus

第九课　读菜单

Dì jiǔ kè　　*Dú càidān*

In this lesson you will learn another fourteen Chinese characters for reading menus.

Fourteen Chinese characters that are basic terms used in menus
Four radicals
Structure of the characters
Practice reading character combinations related to food and drinks
Practice reading signs
Read sample menus
Practice reading sentences
Practice identifying word divisions in a paragraph
Practice writing radicals and characters
Practice writing characters with Chinese word-processing software,
　　using the Pinyin input method

NEW CHARACTERS

冷 lěng	cold, frosty
凉 liáng	cool; cold
冰 bīng	ice, to freeze
红 hóng	red, symbol of luck
白 bái	white, plain
绿 lǜ	green

青 qīng	blue-green, black
黄 huáng	yellow
花 huā	flower, to spend
香 xiāng	fragrant, appetizing
丸 wán	ball, pill, pellet
吃 chī	to eat
店 diàn	shop, store
是 shì	to be (am, is, are, was, were); yes, correct, right

LEARNING RADICALS

Learn these four radicals:

冫 ice	冷 lěng	冰 bīng	次 cì	准 zhǔn
禾 grain	禾 hé	香 xiāng	和 hé	秋 qiū
日 sun	日 rì	早 zǎo	晚 wǎn	春 chūn
冂 borders	肉 ròu	网 wǎng	同 tóng	

冷　冫 (ice R) + 令 lìng (order, cause)

凉　冫 (ice R) + 京 jīng (capital); 京 = 亠 + 口 kǒu (mouth) + 小 xiǎo (little)

冰　冫 (ice R) + 水 shuǐ (water)

红　纟 (silk R) + 工 gōng (work)

白　白 bái (white R)

绿　纟 (silk R) + 录 lù (record); 录 = 彐 + 氺

青　青 qīng (green R); 青 = 龶 + 月 yuè (moon)

黄　八 bā (eight R) + 廿 + 由 yóu (reason)

花　艹 (grass R) + 化 huà (transform); 化 = 亻 + 匕

香　禾 hé (standing grain R) + 日 rì (sun)

丸　丶 (dot R) + 九 jiǔ (nine)

吃　口 kǒu (mouth R) + 乞 qǐ (beg); 乞 = 𠂉 + 乙 yǐ (second)

店　广 guǎng (broad R) + 占 zhàn (occupy);
　　占 = 卜 bǔ (divination) + 口 kǒu (mouth)

是　日 rì (sun R)

READING PRACTICE

1. Read the following words. These are compounds that combine a character from this lesson with other characters you have learned before. Don't memorize the meaning of those words. Try to analyze the meaning of each compound when you read, then look at the English translations given below to check if you get the correct meaning from the reading.

冷　冷饮，冷水，冷茶，冷咖啡

凉　凉菜，凉拌，凉水，凉面，凉丝丝

冰　冰水，冰块，冰啤酒，冰糖，冰冷

红　红茶，红烧，红酒，中国红，红豆

白	白酒，白菜，圆白菜，白糖，炒白菜，辣白菜，白肉，糖醋白菜 白水
绿	绿茶，绿豆
青	青菜，炒青菜，青菜炒肉
黄	黄瓜，黄豆，黄鱼，黄油，黄花菜，黄酱，黄米，黄牛
花	花茶，菜花，绿花菜，花钱
香	香菜，鱼香，香瓜，香油，香港，香水
丸	丸子，肉丸，鱼丸子，炸丸子，蒸丸子
吃	吃素，吃饭，吃奶，白吃，吃不了
店	饭店，酒店，冷饮店，小吃店
是	可是，不是，是不是

English translations:

冷	冷饮 cold drink; 冷水 cold water; 冷茶 cold tea; 冷咖啡 cold coffee
凉	凉菜 cold dish; 凉拌 cold and dressed with sauce; 凉水 cold water; 凉面 cold noodles; 凉丝丝 cool
冰	冰水 ice water; 冰块 ice cube; 冰啤酒 cold beer; 冰糖 rock candy; 冰冷 icy cold

Qínhuái River in Nánjīng

Success with Chinese: Reading & Writing

红　红茶 black tea; 红烧 braised in soy sauce; 红酒 red table wine;
中国红 (name of a famous red wine); 红豆 red beans

白　白酒 spirits; 白菜 Chinese cabbage; 圆白菜 cabbage; 白糖 sugar;
炒白菜 stir-fried cabbage; 辣白菜 spicy Chinese cabbage; 白肉 plain
boiled pork; 糖醋白菜 sweet-and-sour cabbage; 白水 plain water

绿　绿茶 green tea; 绿豆 green beans

青　青菜 green vegetables; 炒青菜 stir-fried green vegetables;
青菜炒肉 stir-fried green vegetables with meat

黄　黄瓜 cucumber; 黄豆 soybean; 黄鱼 yellow croaker; 黄油 butter;
黄花菜 citron day-lily; 黄酱 soybean paste; 黄米 millet;
黄牛 ox, cattle

花　花茶 jasmine tea; 菜花 cauliflower; 绿花菜 broccoli;
花钱 to spend money

香　香菜 coriander; 鱼香 "fish fragrance" (spicy flavor); 香油 sesame oil;
香瓜 casaba; 香港 Hong Kong; 香水 perfume

丸　丸子 ball; 肉丸 meatball; 鱼丸子 fish ball;
炸丸子 deep-fried meatball; 蒸丸子 steamed meatball

吃　吃素 vegetarian; 吃饭 eat a meal; 吃奶 to breastfeed; 白吃 to eat free;
吃不了 can't eat

店　饭店 hotel; 酒店 hotel; 冷饮店 cold drink store;
小吃店 refreshment bar, local snack food restaurant

是　可是 but; 不是 not, it's not; 是不是 Is it? Are they?

2. Read the following signs.

中国大酒店

人民饭店

冷饮店

小吃店

3. Read the following menu of drinks.

MENU	
饮料	
花茶	¥4.00
绿茶	¥4.00
红茶	¥4.00
奶茶	¥15.00
桔汁	¥8.00
白酒	¥25.00
红酒	¥30.00
中国红	¥15.00
冰可乐	¥4.00
冰啤酒	¥8.00
酸奶	¥4.00

4. Read the following sentences.

a. 中国红是红酒。白酒不是wine.

b. 酸奶是饮料。

c. 小吃店可吃小菜，烧饼，油条，炸鸡蛋。

d. 英国人，美国人不吃红烧鱼头。

e. 炒白菜，炒绿花菜，烧豆腐。

f. 一个英国人喝茶，两个美国人喝啤酒。（喝 hē, to drink）
三个中国人喝白酒，四个外国人喝红酒。千百个人不喝
酒。人人都喝牛奶。

5. Read the following menu.

冷菜	
凉拌黄瓜	¥6.50
酸辣白菜	¥8.00
小葱拌豆腐	¥10.00

青菜	
糖醋白菜	¥6.00
炒绿花菜	¥10.00
烧菜花	¥12.00
炒青椒土豆丝	¥5.00

肉菜	
辣子鸡丁	¥16.00
葱头炒肉片	¥12.00
鱼香肉丝	¥15.00
青椒炒肉丝	¥14.00
酱爆肉丁	¥16.00
红烧牛肉	¥20.00
糖醋肉片	¥16.00
鱼香丸子	¥20.00
炸黄鱼	¥26.00
啤酒鸭	¥35.00
酱鸡	¥30.00

汤	
素菜汤	¥6.00
鱼丸汤	¥10.00
鸡蛋汤	¥12.00
酸辣汤	¥8.00

(continued on next page)

米饭	¥1.00
馒头	¥0.50
葱油饼	¥6.00
面条	¥10.00
水饺	¥14.00

6. Underline the characters you can recognize in the following paragraph.

健康饮食让你轻松减肥

怎样吃得健康，有营养，又能保持身材才是最好的。以下几点小建议，就可以让你轻松减肥:

1. 每早空腹喝一大杯温水，可排毒使血液循环更好。
2. 高糖分饮品如汽水，可乐等，每天不可喝超过三杯的可乐，而最后一杯不能在睡前数小时内喝。
3. 避免煎炸及油腻食物，只用少油煮食。
4. 少食多餐，将同样分量的食物分成多次食用。
5. 吃低脂肪的食物，如汤面，白饭，全麦面包等。
6. 每天吃两个水果，如 :桔子，苹果，梨。
7. 少吃含高糖分的食物，如糖果，含糖饮料等。
8. 每天喝八杯水分饮料，多喝清水。

WRITING PRACTICE

Chinese Radical Practice

1. Practice writing these radicals, using the correct stroke order.

冫 _____

冫 _____

冂 _____

冂 _____

禾 _____

禾 _____

日 _____

日 _____

2. In the lines below, write in characters from anywhere in this book that contain the radical given at the start of the row.

冫 _____

冂 _____

禾 _____

日 _____

Chinese Character Practice

Practice writing the following characters by first tracing their outlines, and then writing them on your own. Follow the correct stroke order given here.

| 冷 | 丶 | 冫 | 丷 | 氵 | 氺 | 冷 | 冷 | | | | | | | | | |

| 凉 | 丶 | 冫 | 冫 | 广 | 六 | 泞 | 泞 | 泞 | 泞 | 凉 | | | | | |

| 冰 | 丶 | 冫 | 刂 | 刌 | 冰 | 冰 | | | | | | | | | | |

| 红 | 乚 | 幺 | 纟 | 纟 | 纟 | 红 | 红 | | | | | | | | | |

白 ノ ィ 白 白 白

绿 ㇀ 乚 纟 纩 纩 纴 纥 绿 绿 绿

青 一 二 ㄓ 圭 丰 青 青 青

黄 一 十 卄 共 芇 苄 苗 黄 黄 黄

香 ノ 二 千 禾 禾 禾 香 香 香

花 一 十 卄 艹 芢 花 花

丸 ノ 九 丸

吃 丨 冂 口 吖 吃 吃

店 丶 亠 广 广 庁 庄 店 店

是 丨 冂 日 日 旦 早 早 昰 是

Writing Characters with Chinese Software

Write the following in Chinese characters using the Pinyin input method of your Chinese word-processing program. Alternatively, if you do not have access to a Chinese word-processing program, write out in handwriting the Pinyin with tones and the characters for each of these. The individual characters used in each of the following have been introduced in this lesson or a prior lesson.

1. cold drink
2. red table wine
3. ice cube
4. green tea
5. stir-fried spicy shredded pork with "fish fragrance"
6. stir-fried sliced cabbage with pork
7. fish ball
8. jasmine tea
9. cauliflower and broccoli
10. vegetable oil
11. can't eat any more
12. Hong Kong
13. spend money
14. cold water

10 Telephone

第十课　电话

Dì shí kè　　Diànhuà

In this lesson you will learn fourteen Chinese characters that will help you in making telephone calls in China.

Fourteen Chinese characters that are related to making phone calls
  or shopping
Five radicals
Structure of the characters
Practice reading character combinations related to making phone calls
  or shopping
Practice reading signs
Practice identifying word divisions in a paragraph
Translate sentences from Chinese into English
Practice writing radicals and characters
Practice writing characters with Chinese word-processing software,
  using the Pinyin input method

NEW CHARACTERS

电 diàn	electricity; electric
话 huà	word; to talk
卡 kǎ	card
公 gōng	public, state-owned
用 yòng	to use
手 shǒu	hand

机 jī	machine, engine, opportunity
邮 yóu	post; mail
局 jú	bureau, gathering
商 shāng	business; a surname
买 mǎi	to buy
卖 mài	to sell
在 zài	in, at; to be in, to be at, to exist
有 yǒu	to have

LEARNING RADICALS

Learn these five radicals:

讠 word	话 huà	请 qǐng	谢 xiè	谁 shéi	语 yǔ		
阝 ear (left/right)	邮 yóu	都 dōu	那 nà	哪 nǎ	附 fù		
尸 corpse	尸 shī	局 jú	尺 chǐ	屋 wū	层 céng		
一	买 mǎi	也 yě					
月 moon	月 yuè	有 yǒu	服 fú	肝 gān	肥 féi	肠 cháng	肺 fèi

STRUCTURE OF THE CHARACTERS

Learn the radicals (R) and components of these fourteen Chinese characters:

电　　田 tián (field R) + 乚

话　　讠 (word R) + 舌 shé (tongue); 舌 = 千 qiān + 口 kǒu

卡　　卜 bǔ (divine R) + 下 xià (down, under)

公　　八 bā (eight R) + 厶 (private R)

用　　用 yòng (use R)

手　　手 shǒu (hand R)

机　　木 mù (wood R) + 几 jǐ (few)

邮　　阝 (ear R) + 由 yóu (reason)

局　　尸 shī (corpse R) + 𠃌 + 口 kǒu

商　　亠 (cover R) + ⸯ + 冂 (borders) + 八 bā + 口 kǒu

买　　乛 (R) + 头 tóu (head)

卖　　十 shí (ten R) + 乛 + 头 tóu

在　　土 tǔ (earth R) + 𠂆 + 丨

有　　月 yuè (moon R) + 𠂇

A place to buy phone cards

1. Read the following words. These are compounds that combine a character from this lesson with other characters you have learned before. Don't memorize the meaning of those words. Try to analyze the meaning of each compound when you read, then look at the English translations given below to check if you get the correct meaning from the reading.

电	电子, 电力
话	电话
卡	IC卡, 电话卡, 电子卡, 饭卡
公	公用, 公用电话, 公民, 公牛, 公馆, 公分, 公元
用	用币电话, 用人, 商用, 饮用水, 外用
手	手电, 手头, 手工
机	手机, 卖手机, 电话机, 话机, 商机
邮	邮局, 邮电局, 邮电
局	局面, 电话局, 饭局, 局中人, 局外人
商	商店, 商人, 港商, 台商, 美商, 外商, 面商
买	买饭卡, 买菜, 买饭
卖	买卖, 买卖人, 卖菜, 买卖外币, 外卖, 卖电话卡, 卖国
在	在中国, 在饭店, 在商店, 在邮局, 在外国
有	有人, 有机, 有钱, 有用, 有一手儿, 有面子

English translations:

电	电子 electronic; 电力 electrical power
话	电话 telephone
卡	IC卡 IC card; 电话卡 telephone card; 电子卡 electronic card; 饭卡 meal card
公	公用 public use; 公用电话 pay phone; 公民 citizen; 公牛 bull; 公馆 mansion; 公分 centimeter; 公元 AD, the Christian era

用	用币电话 coin-operated telephone; 用人 to choose a person for a job; 商用 business use; 饮用水 drinking water; 外用 for external use
手	手电 flashlight; 手头 at hand; 手工 hand work
机	手机 mobile phone; 卖手机 to sell mobile phones; 电话机 telephone; 话机 chance for conversation; 商机 business opportunity
邮	邮局 post office; 邮电 post and telecommunications; 邮电局 post office
局	局面 situation; 电话局 telephone exchange; 饭局 dinner gathering; 局中人 player; 局外人 outsider
商	商店 store; 商人 businessperson; 港商 Hong Kong businessperson; 美商 American businessperson; 台商 Taiwan businessperson; 外商 foreign businessperson; 面商 to discuss face to face
买	买饭卡 to buy a meal card; 买菜 to buy vegetables; 买饭 to buy a meal
卖	买卖 to buy and sell; 买卖人 businesspeople; 卖菜 to sell vegetables; 卖电话卡 to sell a phone card; 外卖 to sell take-out food; 买卖外币 to buy and sell foreign currency; 卖国 to betray one's country
在	在中国 in China; 在饭店 at a hotel; 在商店 in the store; 在邮局 in the post office; 在外国 in a foreign country
有	有钱 rich; 有人 there is someone; 有机 organic; 有用 useful; 有一手儿 have a remarkable skill; 有面子 gain face, have the honor

2. Read the following signs.

公用电话

卖手机

电子城 (chéng, city)

邮局

電話卡

IC卡電話

用幣電話

3. Underline the characters you recognize in the following paragraph.

卡式电话从八十年代中期开始进入中国的公用电话网。
1985年，中国最早的电话卡出现于深圳市。按电话卡的
储值方式，在我国使用过或正在使用的主要有以下几类：

A. 磁卡（Magnetic Strip Card）：这种卡使用最广泛，

B. IC卡：又叫智慧卡（Chip Card），电子卡（Electronic Card），1984年
由法国发明。卡上有集成电路（IC晶片）存储金额信息，
可回收使用。5年后，IC卡将成为中国电话卡的主流。

C. IP电话卡：是国内使用长途预付费和密码记帐相结合的
电话卡。最早在广东使用时叫200电话卡，在南京叫 "9989"
信息卡，在上海叫 "信息卡"。

4. Translate the following sentences into English.

a. 商店卖手机和电话卡。（和 hé, and）

b. 邮局可用IC卡电话。酒店可用电话卡。

c. 商人用手机。

d. 银行买卖外币。

e. 公用电话不用电话卡。

f. 食堂用饭卡吃饭。饭店用钱吃饭。

g. 美国用美圆，英国用英镑，香港用港币，中国用人民
币，欧洲用欧元。

（香港 Xiānggǎng, Hong Kong; 欧洲 Ōuzhōu, Europe）

Chinese Radical Practice

1. Practice writing these radicals, using the correct stroke order.

讠 _____

讠 _____

阝 _____

阝 _____

尸 _____

尸 _____

⼀ _____

一 _____

月 _____

月 _____

2. In the lines below, write in characters from anywhere in this book that contain the radical given at the start of the row.

讠 _____

阝 _____

尸 _____

一 _____

月 _____

Chinese Character Practice

Practice writing the following characters by first tracing their outlines, and then writing them on your own. Follow the correct stroke order given here.

| 电 | 丶 | 冂 | 曰 | 日 | 电 | | | | | | | | | | |

| 话 | 丶 | 讠 | 讠 | 讠 | 讠 | 讠 | 话 | 话 | | | | | | | |

| 卡 | 丨 | 卜 | 上 | 卡 | 卡 | | | | | | | | | | |

| 公 | 丿 | 八 | 公 | 公 | | | | | | | | | | | |

| 用 | 丿 | 冂 | 月 | 月 | 用 | | | | | | | | | | |

| 手 | 一 | 二 | 三 | 手 | | | | | | | | | | | |

| 机 | 一 | 十 | 才 | 木 | 朾 | 机 | | | | | | | | | |

| 邮 | 丶 | 冂 | 曰 | 由 | 由 | 由阝 | 邮 | | | | | | | | |

| 局 | 乛 | 丿 | 尸 | 吊 | 吊 | 局 | 局 | | | | | | | | |

| 商 | 丶 | 亠 | 产 | 产 | 产 | 产 | 产 | 商 | 商 | 商 | | | | | |

| 买 | 乛 | 乛 | 乛 | 丒 | �买 | 买 | | | | | | | | | |

| 卖 | 一 | 十 | 士 | 士 | 卡 | 壴 | 卖 | 卖 | | | | | | | |

| 在 | 一 | 厂 | 才 | 右 | 在 | 在 | | | | | | | | | |

| 有 | 一 | 广 | 才 | 冇 | 有 | 有 | | | | | | | | | |

Writing Characters with Chinese Software

Write the following in Chinese characters using the Pinyin input method of your Chinese word-processing program. Alternatively, if you do not have access to a Chinese word-processing program, write out in handwriting the Pinyin with tones and the characters for each of these. The individual characters used in each of the following have been introduced in this lesson or a prior lesson.

1. telephone
2. telephone card
3. pay phone
4. coin-operated telephone
5. centimeter
6. store
7. businessperson
8. discuss face to face
9. post office
10. buy and sell
11. to sell take out
12. mobile phone
13. flashlight
14. business opportunity

11

Hotels

第十一课　宾馆

Dì shíyī kè　　*Bīnguǎn*

In this lesson you will learn fourteen Chinese characters that will help you read signs in Chinese hotels.

Fourteen Chinese characters that are related to hotels
Four radicals
Structure of the characters
Practice reading character combinations related to hotels
Practice reading signs
Practice reading sentences
Practice writing radicals and characters
Practice writing characters with Chinese word-processing software, using the Pinyin input method

NEW CHARACTERS

宾 bīn	guest
房 fáng	room, house
间 jiān	room; between
单 dān	single, bill
双 shuāng	double, twin, pair
上 shàng	first, upper; to go up, to get on

下 xià	to go down; get off; down, under, below; next
楼 lóu	multi-story building; story, floor
厕 cè	toilet
所 suǒ	place; measure word (buildings)
男 nán	man, male
女 nǚ	woman, female
洗 xǐ	to wash
号 hào	number, size; date

LEARNING RADICALS

Learn these four radicals:

方 **square**	方 fāng	房 fáng	旁 páng	旅 lǚ		
门 **door**	门 mén	间 jiān	问 wèn	们 mén		
宀 **roof**	宾 bīn	客 kè	室 shì	字 zì		
厂 **factory**	厂 chǎng	厕 cè	厅 tīng	厨 chú	历 lì	厉 lì

STRUCTURE OF THE CHARACTERS

Learn the radicals (R) and components of these fourteen Chinese characters:

宾　宀 (roof R) + 兵 bīng (soldier)　兵 = 八 bā (eight R)

房　户 hù (household R) + 方 fāng (square); 户 = 丶 + 尸 shī (corpse);

　　方 = 丶 + 万 wàn (ten thousand)

间　门 mén (door R) + 日 rì (sun)

单　丷 (R) + 田 tián (field) + 十 shí (ten)

双　又 yòu (again R) + 又

上　一 yī (one R)

下　一 yī (one R)

楼　木 mù (wood R) + 米 mǐ (rice) + 女 nǚ (woman)

厕　厂 chǎng (plant R) + 则 zé (standard); 则 = 贝 bèi (shell) + 刂 (knife R)

所　户 hù (household R) + 斤 jīn (0.5 kilo)

男　田 tián (field R) + 力 lì (power)

女　女 nǚ (woman R)

洗　氵 (water R) + 先 xiān (first); 先 = 生 + 儿 ér (son)

号　口 kǒu (mouth R) + 丂 kē (a phonetic symbol used in Taiwan)

READING PRACTICE

1. Read the following words. These are compounds that combine a character from this lesson with other characters you have learned before. Don't memorize the meaning of those words. Try to analyze the meaning of each compound when you read, then look at the English translations given below to check if you get the correct meaning from the reading.

宾　宾馆, 外宾, 国宾, 国宾馆

房　房子, 公房

间　房间, 中间, 一间

单	单间，单人间，买单，菜单，单元，单元房，四单元，单子
双	双人间，双手，双十，一双
上	上宾，上饭馆，上饭，上手，上火
下	下饭，下酒菜，下蛋，下面，下面条，可上可下，上下
楼	楼房，三楼，楼上，楼下，上楼，下楼
厕	厕所，女厕，男厕，公厕，毛厕
所	女厕所，男厕所，所有，所在，一所宾馆
男	男人，男子，男角
女	女人，女子，男女，男男女女，女角，子女
洗	洗手，洗手间，洗头，洗菜
号	五号楼，电话号，手机号，小号，中号，大号

English translations:

宾	宾馆 hotel; 外宾 foreign guest; 国宾 state guest; 国宾馆 state guest house
房	房子 house; 公房 public house
间	房间 room; 中间 middle; 一间 one room
单	单间 single room; 单人间 single room; 买单 bill; 菜单 menu; 单元 unit; 单元房 apartment; 四单元 apartment unit four; 单子 list, bill
双	双人间 double room; 双手 two hands; 双十 October 10; 一双 a pair
上	上宾 guest of honor; 上饭馆 go to a restaurant; 上饭 serve the meal; 上手 left-hand seat, start; 上火 get angry
下	下饭 (dishes) to go with rice; 下酒菜 (dishes) to go with wine; 下蛋 lay an egg; 下面 below; 下面条 cook noodles; 可上可下 be able to go up or down; 上下 up and down

楼　楼房 building; 三楼 third floor; 楼上 upstairs; 楼下 downstairs; 上楼 go upstairs; 下楼 go downstairs

厕　厕所 toilet; 女厕 ladies' room; 男厕 men's room; 公厕 public bathroom; 毛厕 public bathroom

所　女厕所 ladies' room; 男厕所 men's room; 所有 own; 所在 location; 一所宾馆 one hotel

男　男人 man; 男子 male; 男角 actor

女　女人 woman; 女子 female; 男女 men and women; 男男女女 men and women; 女角 actress; 子女 children

洗　洗手 wash hands; 洗手间 washroom; 洗头 wash hair; 洗菜 wash vegetables

号　五号楼 Building #5; 电话号 telephone number; 手机号 mobile phone number; 小号 small size; 中号 medium size; 大号 large size

2. Read the following signs.

公厕

洗手间

男厕

女厕

邮电宾馆

三元酒店

九单元

菜单

3. Find the different room prices in the chart.

房间单价（dānjià, price）	
单人间	600 元
双人间	350 元
标准间 (biāozhǔn, standard)	280 元
套间 (tào, suite, set)	1,200 元

4. Read the following sentences.

a. 订一间双人间。 (订 dìng, reserve, book)

b. 小姐，买单。 (小姐 xiǎojiě, Miss)

c. 手机号和电话号在房间里。 (里 lǐ, inside)

d. 宾馆里有中餐馆，菜单上有红烧鱼，辣子鸡，素菜，下酒菜。

e. 四单元六门604号。

f. 外宾在三楼301房间，电话是8759-9534。

g. 女人用女厕所，男人用男厕所，人人都用洗手间。

WRITING PRACTICE

Chinese Radical Practice

1. Practice writing these radicals, using the correct stroke order.

方 _____

方 _____

门 _____

门 _____

宀 _____

宀 _____

厂 _____

厂 _____

2. In the lines below, write in characters from anywhere in this book that contain the radical given at the start of the row.

方 _____

门 _____

宀 _____

厂 _____

Chinese Character Practice

Practice writing the following characters by first tracing their outlines, and then writing them on your own. Follow the correct stroke order given here.

宾	丶	宀	宀	宀	宀	宀	宀	宾	宾						

房	丶	宀	宀	户	户	户	房	房							

间	丨	冂	门	门	问	问	间								

单	丶	丷	丷	屵	屵	甴	旦	单							

双	又	又	刃	双											

上	丨	卜	上												

下	一	丁	下												

Writing Characters with Chinese Software

Write the following in Chinese characters using the Pinyin input method of your Chinese word-processing program. Alternatively, if you do not have access to a Chinese word-processing program, write out in handwriting the Pinyin with tones and the characters for each of these. The individual characters used in each of the following have been introduced in this lesson or a prior lesson.

1. Hong Kong Hotel
2. single room, double room
3. Men drink spirits; women drink red wine.
4. State guests are on the first floor, room 1102.
5. The phone number is 759-9534.
6. The foreign guest is in Apartment Building 5, door 3, room 201.
7. There is a bathroom one hundred meters away.
8. The restaurant is upstairs.
9. Go downstairs to buy a phone card.
10. The foreign guest has a mobile phone.
11. Miss, the check please.
12. There are women and men in the room.
13. The menu has stir-fried spicy diced pork and stewed fish slices.
14. Go to the restaurant to eat.

12

Signs & Directions (1)
第十二课　路标方向(一)

Dì shíèr kè　　*Lùbīao fāngxiàng*

 In this lesson you will learn fourteen Chinese characters that frequently appear in directional signs and street names.

Fourteen Chinese characters that are used in signs and street names
Four radicals
Structure of the characters
Practice reading combinations of characters
Practice reading signs and street names
Practice reading sentences
Practice writing radicals and characters
Practice writing characters with Chinese word-processing software,
　　using the Pinyin input method

NEW CHARACTERS

前 qián	front; forward; in front of; preceding
后 hòu	rear, back, the latter; behind, after
左 zuǒ	left
右 yòu	right
旁 páng	side; nearby; other
边 biān	side, edge

往 wàng/wǎng	to go; toward, in the direction of
大 dà	big, large, major; age
马 mǎ	horse
路 lù	road; route, journey
对 duì	opposite; right, correct
过 guò	to pass, to cross; to celebrate, spend (time), to go through
里 lǐ	inside, inner; a Chinese unit of length
转 zhuǎn/zhuàn	to turn; to change; to rotate

LEARNING RADICALS

Learn these four radicals:

又 **also**	又 yòu	对 duì	双 shuāng	友 yǒu	难 nán				
工 **work**	工 gōng	左 zuǒ	差 chā	功 gōng					
辶 **walk**	边 biān	过 guò	通 tōng	道 dào	近 jìn	进 jìn	这 zhè	还 huái	送 sòng
𧾷 **foot**	足 zú	路 lù	跟 gēn						

STRUCTURE OF THE CHARACTERS

Learn the radicals (R) and components of these twelve Chinese characters:

前　丷 (R) + 一 yī (one) + 月 yuè (moon) + 刂 (knife)

后　丿 (left-falling stroke R) + 一 yī (one) + 口 kǒu (mouth)

左　工 gōng (work R) + 𠂇

右　口 kǒu (mouth R) + 𠂇

旁　方 fāng (square R) + 亠 + 丷 + 冖

边　辶 (walk R) + 力 lì (power)

往　彳 (step R) + 主 zhǔ (host)

大　大 dà (big R)

马　马 mǎ (horse R)

路　𧾷 (food R) + 各 gè (each)　　各 = 夂 + 口 kǒu (mouth)

对　又 yòu (again R) + 寸 cùn (1/10 meter)

过　辶 (walk R) + 寸 cùn (1/10 meter)

里　里 lǐ (inside R)

转　车 chē (vehicle R) + 专 zhuān (expert)

READING PRACTICE

1. Read the following words. These are compounds that combine a character from this lesson with other characters you have learned before. Don't memorize the meaning of those words. Try to analyze the meaning of each compound when you read, then look at the English translations given below to check if you get the correct meaning from the reading.

前　前面, 前人

后　后面, 前后, 后人, 后头

左　左面, 左右, 左手

右　右面, 右手, 前后左右

旁　旁人, 两旁

边　旁边，前边，后边，左边，右边，一边，两边，边卡

往　往前，前往，往日，往往，往后，往上

大　大白菜，大饼，大葱，大小，大半，大号，大吃大喝，
大，鱼大肉，大男大女，大有人在，大鱼吃小鱼，大局

马　马，小马，马房，牛马，马上，下马

路　路边，马路，路口，大路，公路，小路，路人，路面，
路子 后路

对　对面，对过，对虾，对外，对话，对手，对头，一对

过　过马路，路过，过路人，过往，过分，过日子 吃过了

里　里边，里面，里头，里外，里里外外

转　转角，左转，右转，往右转，转卖，转手，转口，转换

English translations:

前　前面 in front; 前人 predecessor

后　后面 behind; 前后 around, from start to finish; 后人 descendants;
后头 the back

左　左面 left side; 左右 left and right, about; 左手 the left hand

右　右面 right side; 右手 the right hand; 前后左右 all sides

旁　旁人 other people; 两旁 both sides

边　旁边 side, nearby; 前边 front; 后边 rear; 左边 left side; 右边 right
side; 一边 one side; 两边 both sides; 边卡 border checkpoint

往　往前 go forward; 前往 leave for; 往日 in the past; 往往 often;
往后 from now on; 往上 go uphill

大　大白菜 Chinese cabbage; 大饼 large flat bread; 大葱 Chinese green
onion; 大小 size, big or small; 大半 more than half; 大号 large size;
大吃大喝 spend lavishly on feasting; 大鱼大肉 rich food;
大男大女 old maid and old bachelor; 大有人在 there are plenty of such
people; 大鱼吃小鱼 the strong prey on the weak; 大局 overall situation

马	马 horse; 小马 pony; 马房 stable; 牛马 beasts of burden;
	马上 immediately; 下马 be discontinued
路	路边 curb; 马路 road; 路口 intersection; 大路 broad road;
	公路 highway; 小路 trail; 路人 passerby, stranger; 路面 road surface;
	路子 way; 后路 route of retreat
对	对面 opposite; 对过 across the way; 对虾 prawn; 对外 external;
	对话 have a dialogue; 对手 opponent; 对头 correct, enemy; 一对 a pair
过	过马路 to cross a street; 路过 pass by; 过路人 passerby;
	过往 come and go; 过分 excessive; 过日子 live; 吃过了 have eaten
里	里边 inside; 里面 inside; 里头 inside; 里外 inside and outside;
	里里外外 inside and outside
转	转角 corner; 左转 turn left; 右转 turn right; 往右转 turn toward
	right; 转卖 resell; 转手 pass on; 转口 transit; 转换 transform

2. Read the following signs.

往前一百米有厕所

前面路口不可右转

单行路

五号公路

3. Read the following street names.

百乐路
国宾路
大红门路
人民大路
三元里
人大前里

A street sign offers directions

4. Read the following sentences.

a. 大路旁边有一个宾馆,宾馆里有厕所。

b. 马路右边有一个冷饮店,卖冰啤酒。

c. 往前，过了中国银行，往左转有一个邮局。邮局里卖
电话卡。

d. 马路对过有一个餐馆卖大饼和炸大虾。

e. 有一个路人在马路对面前后左右转。

f. 男男女女中，大吃大喝的人，大有人在；大鱼吃小鱼的
人，大有人在；有一手儿的人，也大有人在。(的 de, that, who)

WRITING PRACTICE

Chinese Radical Practice

1. Practice writing these radicals, using the correct stroke order.

又 _____

又 _____

工 _____

工 _____

辶 _____

辶 _____

足 _____

足 _____

2. In the lines below, write in characters from anywhere in this book that contain the radical given at the start of the row.

又 _____

工 _____

辶 _____

足 _____

Chinese Character Practice

Practice writing the following characters by first tracing their outlines, and then writing them on your own. Follow the correct stroke order given here.

| 前 | 丶 | 丷 | 丷 | 广 | 刅 | 刅 | 肙 | 前 | 前 | | | | | | | | | |

| 后 | ´ | 厂 | 厂 | 斤 | 后 | 后 | | | | | | | | | |

| 左 | 一 | ナ | ナ | 左 | 左 | | | | | | | |

| 右 | 一 | ナ | ナ | 右 | 右 | | | | | | | |

| 旁 | 丶 | 亠 | 亠 | 亠 | 亠 | 亠 | 亠 | 亭 | 旁 | | | | | | |

| 边 | フ | カ | カ | 边 | 边 | | | | | | | |

| 往 | ´ | 彡 | 彳 | 彳 | 彳 | 彳 | 往 | 往 | | | | | | | |

| 大 | 一 | ナ | 大 | | | | | | | | | | | | | |

| 马 | フ | 马 | 马 | | | | | | | | | | | | |

Writing Characters with Chinese Software

Write the following in Chinese characters using the Pinyin input method of your Chinese word-processing program. Alternatively, if you do not have access to a Chinese word-processing program, write out in handwriting the Pinyin with tones and the characters for each of these. The individual characters used in each of the following have been introduced in this lesson or a prior lesson.

1. in front of the Hong Kong Hotel

2. both sides of the room

3. The man's room is on the right; the woman's room is on the left.

4. in the direction of the State Guest House

5. After passing the bank, go forward.

6. behind the apartment building

7. Turn right, and there is a bathroom one hundred meters away.

8. The restaurant is upstairs.

9. Immediately cross the street.

10. Turn right, and pass by the corner.

11. highway intersection

12. There are plenty of such people eating rich food.

13. There are salesmen selling Chinese cabbage everywhere.

14. There is a bathroom inside the hotel.

13

Signs & Directions (2)
第十三课　路标方向(二)
Dì shísān kè　　*Lùbiāo fāngxiàng*

In this lesson you will learn fourteen Chinese characters that will help you to read signs and directions.

Fourteen Chinese characters that are used in signs and directions
Four radicals
Structure of the characters
Practice reading character combinations
Practice reading signs
Practice reading an announcement and sentences
Practice writing radicals and characters
Practice writing characters with Chinese word-processing software,
　using the Pinyin input method

NEW CHARACTERS

文 wén	literature; writing
系 xì	department (in a college)
门 mén	entrance, door, gate
教 jiāo/jiào	to teach
学 xué	to study, to learn; school, knowledge
图 tú	picture, map

书 shū	book, document; to write
办 bàn	to manage, to handle, to set up
室 shì	room; office
地 dì	earth, locality, field
网 wǎng	net, Internet
吧 bā/ba	bar, cafe; (particle) to make a mild imperative, to imply agreement or a degree of certainty, to express unwillingness or hesitation
直 zhí	(particle) straight; vertical; frank
走 zǒu	to walk, to go, to leave

LEARNING RADICALS

Learn these four radicals:

文 literature	教 jiāo	数 shù	修 xiū	各 gè
子 / 孑 child	子 zǐ	学 xué	孩 hái	字 zì
力 power	力 lì	办 bàn	加 jiā	男 nán
卜 divination	卜 bǔ	卡 kǎ	外 wài	占 zhàn

Learn the radicals (R) and components of these twelve Chinese characters:

文　文 wén (literary R)

系　丿 (R) + 糸 = 幺 yāo (youngest) + 小 xiǎo (little)

门　门 mén (door R)

教　攵 (literary R) + 孝 xiào (filial piety)

学　子 zǐ (child R)

图　囗 (enclosure R) + 冬 dōng (winter); 冬 = 夂 + 冫

书　一 (R)

办　力 lì (power R)

室　宀 (roof R) + 至 zhì (one); 至 = 一 + 厶 + 土

地　土 tǔ (earth R) + 也 yě (also)

网　冂 (borders R) + ㄨㄨ

吧　口 kǒu (mouth R) + 巴 bā (cling to)

直　十 shí (ten R) + 且 qiě (just, even)

走　走 zǒu (walk R)

1. Read the following words. These are compounds that combine a character from this lesson with other characters you have learned before. Don't memorize the meaning of those words. Try to analyze the meaning of each compound when you read, then look at the English translations given below to check if you get the correct meaning from the reading.

文　文人, 中文, 英文, 外文, 文学

系　中文系, 英文系, 文学系, 外文系, 图书馆系

门　门口, 大门, 前门, 后门, 门面, 门里, 门外,
　　门房, 门路

教　教学, 教室, 教堂, 教条, 四教, 文教

学	小学, 中学, 大学, 学中文, 学英文, 文学, 学前
图	图书, 图书馆, 图片, 图钱
书	书店, 书局, 书房, 书商, 书单, 书后, 书面, 教书, 文书, 国书
办	办公, 办公室, 办公楼, 办公大楼, 办学
室	室外, 室中, 教室, 315室, 中文系办公室
地	地图, 地面, 地下, 地下室, 地方, 地头, 地瓜
网	网吧, 上网, 电网, 鱼网
吧	酒吧, 酒吧间, 吃吧
直	一直, 一直上, 一直下, 一直往前, 口直
走	走路, 一直走, 往前走, 走过, 走后门, 走吧

English translations:

文	文人 scholar; 中文 Chinese; 英文 English; 外文 foreign languages; 文学 literature
系	中文系 Chinese Department; 英文系 English Department; 文学系 Literature Department; 外文系 Foreign Languages Department; 图书馆系 Librarianship Department
门	门口 entrance; 大门 main gate; 前门 front door; 后门 back door; 门面 shop front; 门里 inside the door; 门外 outside the door; 门房 doorman; 门路 social connections
教	教学 teaching; 教室 classroom; 教堂 church; 教条 doctrine; 四教 #4 classroom building; 文教 culture and education
学	小学 elementary school; 中学 secondary school; 大学 university, college; 学中文 study Chinese; 学英文 study English; 文学 literature; 学前 preschool
图	图书 books; 图书馆 library; 图片 picture, photo; 图钱 to pursue wealth

书　书店 bookstore; 书局 publishing house; 书房 study; 书商 book merchant; 书单 book list; 书后 postscript; 书面 in written form; 教书 to teach; 文书 copy clerk, secretary; 国书 credentials presented to the head of a foreign state

办　办公 work in an office; 办公室 office; 办公楼 office building; 办公大楼 large office building; 办学 run a school

室　室外 outside; 室中 inside room; 教室 classroom; 315室 room 315; 中文系办公室 Chinese Department office

地　地图 map; 地面 ground; 地下 underground; 地下室 basement; 地方 place, local; 地头 edge of a field; 地瓜 yam, sweet potato

网　网吧 Internet cafe; 上网 get on the Internet; 电网 electrified barbed wire; 鱼网 fishnet

吧　酒吧 bar; 酒吧间 bar; 吃吧 please eat

直　一直 straight; 一直上 go straight up; 一直下 go straight down; 一直往前 go straight ahead; 口直 straightforward

走　走路 go on foot; 一直走 go straight; 往前走 go forward; 走过 go through; 走后门 get something done through the "back door"; 走吧 let's go

Hong Kong

2. Read the following signs.

外文系办公室

红文中学

图书馆

第四教学楼

中国文学系

外文书店

英文系教室请上三楼

网吧在地下室

3. Read the following announcement.

通知

宾馆前台可换外币。上网请到商务中心。在房间上网请
到前台开通网路。西餐厅在一楼，中餐厅在二楼。

新园宾馆

4. Read the following sentences.

a. 英文系旁边是中文系。

b. 外文书店在马路对面，邮局和银行中间。

c. 网吧一直往前走，过了教学楼，往右转，在图书馆旁
边。

d. 中文系在办公楼的前边，不在后边。

e. 大门口右边有一个餐馆，左边有一个网吧，对面是宾
馆。

f. 银行里有美圆。邮局里有电话。宾馆里有外宾。饭馆里有鸡鸭鱼肉，有酒有菜。

g. 小学，中学，大学都是学校 (xuéxiào, school)，是不是？

Chinese Radical Practice

1. Practice writing these radicals, using the correct stroke order.

夂 _____

夂 _____

孑 _____

子 _____

力 _____

力 _____

卜 _____

卜 _____

2. In the lines below, write in characters from anywhere in this book that contain the radical given at the start of the row.

夂 _____

子 _____

力 _____

卜 _____

Chinese Character Practice

Practice writing the following characters by first tracing their outlines, and then writing them on your own. Follow the correct stroke order given here.

文　`　二　宁　文

系　一　乡　乡　玄　乡　系　系

门　`　门　门

教　一　十　土　耂　耂　孝　孝　孝　教　教　教

学　`　`　`　`　兴　学　学　学

图　l　冂　门　冈　冈　罔　图　图

书　乛　乛　书　书

办　フ　力　办　办

室　`　宀　宀　宀　宊　宝　室　室

地　一　十　土　圫　地　地

网　l　冂　冂　冈　冈　网

吧　l　口　口　叮　叭　吧　吧

直　一　十　广　古　古　直　直　直

走　一　十　土　丰　走　走　走

　　　　　Success with Chinese: Reading & Writing

Writing Characters with Chinese Software

Write the following in Chinese characters using the Pinyin input method of your Chinese word-processing program. Alternatively, if you do not have access to a Chinese word-processing program, write out in handwriting the Pinyin with tones and the characters for each of these. The individual characters used in each of the following have been introduced in this lesson or a prior lesson.

1. teaching English in the English Department
2. Foreign Languages School
3. university main gate
4. study Chinese in the Chinese Department
5. The library has books and maps.
6. Book merchants sell books at bookstores.
7. elementary school, secondary school, and university
8. working in the office in a large office building
9. getting on the Internet at the Internet cafe
10. Drinking beer, red wine, and spirits at the bar.
11. People are inside and outside the classroom.
12. #4 classroom building
13. The doorman is at the entrance.
14. There is an Internet cafe in the basement.

14 Signs & Directions (3)

第十四课　路标方向(三)

Dì shísì kè　　　Lùbiāo fāngxiàng

In this lesson you will learn to read and write sixteen Chinese characters that will help you to read signs and directions.

Sixteen Chinese characters that are used in signs and directions
Four radicals
Structure of the characters
Practice reading character combinations
Practice reading signs and street names
Practice reading sentences and paragraphs
Practice writing radicals and characters
Practice writing characters with Chinese word-processing software,
　　using the Pinyin input method

NEW CHARACTERS

东 dōng	east
西 xī	west
南 nán	south
北 běi	north
街 jiē	street
通 tōng	to lead to, to go through; to open
道 dào	road, channel

入 rù	to enter, to join
进 jìn	to enter, to come in
出 chū	go out, exit; appear
京 jīng	capital; [Beijing]
市 shì	market; city
请 qǐng	please; invite
勿 wù	don't
由 yóu	reason; through
此 cǐ	here, this

LEARNING RADICALS

Learn these four radicals:

匕 spoon	匕 bǐ	北 běi	比 bǐ	化 huà
亻 man	你 nǐ	他 tā	们 mén	什 shén
巾 towel	巾 jīn	市 shì	币 bì	
勹 wrap	勿 wù	勺 sháo	包 bāo	句 jù

Success with Chinese: Reading & Writing

Learn the radicals (R) and components of these sixteen Chinese characters:

东 — 一 yī (one R) + 乙 + 小 xiǎo (little)

西 — 一 yī (one R) + 儿 + 口

南 — 十 shí (ten R)

北 — 匕 bǐ (an ancient type of spoon R)

街 — 彳 (step R) + 土 + 土 + 一 + 丁

通 — 辶 (walk R) + 甬 yǒng (name of a city); 甬 = マ + 用 yòng (use)

道 — 辶 (walk R) + 首 shǒu (head) 首 = 丷 + 一 + 自

入 — 人 rén (person R)

进 — 辶 (walk R) + 井 jǐng (well)

出 — 凵 (R)

京 — 亠 (cover R) + 口 + 小 xiǎo (little)

市 — 亠 (cover R) + 巾 jīn (towel)

请 — 讠 (word R) + 青 qīng (blue-green); 青 = 丰 + 月 yuè (moon)

勿 — 勹 (wrap R)

由 — 由 yóu (reason R)

此 — 止 zhǐ (stop R) + 匕 bǐ (an ancient type of spoon)

1. Read the following words. These are compounds that combine a character from this lesson with other characters you have learned before. Don't memorize the meaning of those words. Try to analyze the meaning of each compound when you read, then look at the English translations given below to check if you get the correct meaning from the reading.

东 — 东边, 东北, 东南, 东面, 东北角, 东南角, 东大街, 东门, 路东, 往东, 东欧

西 — 西边, 西面, 西北, 西南, 西北角, 西南角, 西街,

	西大街, 西门, 东西, 路西, 往西, 西欧, 西餐
南	南边, 南面, 南门, 路南, 往南, 南国, 南美
北	北边, 北面, 北街, 北门, 路北, 往北, 东西南北, 北京, 北京大学（北大）, 北国, 北美
街	大街, 小街, 街道, 街头, 南大街, 北大街, 过街, 前街, 后街
通	通往, 通行, 通过, 通道, 左通道, 南通道, 过街通道
道	道路, 大道, 国道, 过道, 道人
入	入口, 入学, 入港, 入手, 入门, 入木三分
进	进口, 进入, 进大学, 进料, 买进, 进行
出	出口, 进出, 进出口, 出门, 出国, 出面, 出卖, 出路, 出马出头, 出手, 出局, 出走
京	北京, 南京, 东京, 北京路, 南京路
市	北京市, 南京市, 东京市, 书市, 菜市, 市民, 市中心
请	请进, 请人, 请教, 请吃, 请上楼
勿	勿用, 勿饮, 请勿, 勿进, 请勿进入, 请勿饮用
由	由头
此	由此, 由此过马路, 由此上, 由此下, 由此往东

English translations:

东	东边 east side; 东北 northeast; 东南 southeast; 东面 east side; 东北角 northeast corner; 东南角 southeast corner; 东大街 East Street; 东门 east gate; 路东 east side of the road; 往东 toward the east; 东欧 Eastern Europe
西	西边 west side; 西面 west side; 西北 northwest; 西南 southwest; 西北角 northwest corner; 西南角 southwest corner; 西街 West Street; 西大街 West Street; 西门 west gate; 路西 west side of the road; 往西 toward the west; 西欧 Western Europe; 西餐 Western-style food; 东西 thing

南	南边 south side; 南面 south side; 南门 south gate; 路南 south side of the road; 往南 toward the south; 南国 the South; 南美 South America
北	北边 north side; 北面 north side; 北街 North Street; 北门 north gate; 路北 north side of the road; 往北 toward north; 东西南北 the four directions; 北京 Beijing; 北京大学（北大）Beijing University (Běidà); 北国 the North; 北美 North America
街	大街 a main street; 小街 alley; 街道 neighborhood; 街头 street corner; 南大街 South Street; 北大街 North Street; 过街 cross street; 前街 Front Street; 后街 Rear Street
通	通行 pass through; 通过 go through; 通道 passageway; 左通道 left passageway; 南通道 south passageway; 过街通道 pedestrian tunnel; 直通 go straight to
道	道路 road; 大道 main road; 国道 interstate highway; 过道 hallway; 道人 Taoist priest
入	入口 entrance; 入学 enter a school; 入港 enter a port; 入手 begin with; 入门 learn the rudiments of a subject; 入木三分 penetrating
进	进口 import; 进入 enter; 进大学 enter a university; 进料 stock with materials; 买进 buy in; 进行 be in the process of
出	出口 export; 进出 in and out; 进出口 import-export; 出门 go out; 出国 go abroad; 出面 on behalf of; 出卖 betray; 出路 the way out; 出马 go into action; 出头 free oneself from misery, come forward; 出手 dispose of; 出局 out of the game; 出走 run away
京	北京 Beijing; 南京 Nanjing; 东京 Tokyo; 北京路 Beijing Road; 南京路 Nanjing Road
市	北京市 Beijing City; 南京市 Nanjing City; 东京市 Tokyo City; 书市 book market; 菜市 vegetable market; 市民 city residents; 市中心 downtown

请	请人 hire people; 请教 consult; 请吃 please eat; 请上楼 please go upstairs
勿	勿用 don't use; 勿饮 don't drink; 请勿 please don't; 勿进 don't go in; 请勿进入 please don't enter; 请勿饮用 please don't drink
由	由头 pretext, reason
此	由此 from this; 由此过马路 cross the street from here; 由此上 go up from here; 由此下 go down from here; 由此往东 go towards the east from here

2. Read the following signs.

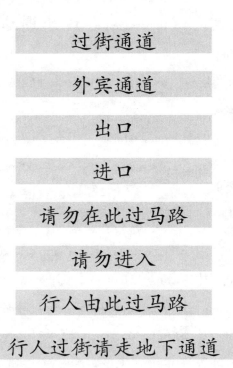

过街通道

外宾通道

出口

进口

请勿在此过马路

请勿进入

行人由此过马路

行人过街请走地下通道

3. Read the following street names.

西直门大街	牛街
西单北大街	菜市口
东门路	中英街
南京路	十二条

4. Read the following sentences.

a. 前门东大街在前门东边。前门西大街在前门西边。

b. 菜市口不是菜市。菜市在宾馆后面。

c. 过了书市一直往前走，在路口往右转，是外语大学。

d. 东门在东门路，有很多商店，卖很多东西。(很多 hěn duō, many)

e. 西单大街东北角有一个西餐馆，东南角有一个网吧。

f. 有一个商人在大学对面的马路边卖东西。他卖可乐，啤酒，冰水和吃的东西。他后面有一个牌子写着："请勿在马路两边买卖东西"。(他 tā, he; 牌子 páizi, sign; 写着 xiězhe, writes)

g. 南京大学在南京市。大学里有英文系，中文系，图书馆系。英文系教英国文学和美国文学。中文系教中国文学。图书馆系不在图书馆里。学校里有餐馆，商店，银行，邮局和书店。

WRITING PRACTICE

Chinese Radical Practice

1. Practice writing these radicals, using the correct stroke order.

匕 _____

匕 _____

亻 _____

亻 _____

巾 _____

巾 _____

勺 _____

勹 _____

2. In the lines below, write in characters from anywhere in this book that contain the radical given at the start of the row.

匕 _____

亻 _____

巾 _____

勹 _____

Chinese Character Practice

Practice writing the following characters by first tracing their outlines, and then writing them on your own. Follow the correct stroke order given here.

| 东 | 一 | 七 | 乔 | 夯 | 东 | | | | | | | | |

| 西 | 一 | 丆 | 冂 | 襾 | 西 | 西 | | | | | | | |

| 南 | 一 | 十 | 冂 | 内 | 内 | 内 | 南 | 南 | 南 | | | | |

| 北 | 一 | 十 | 扌 | 北 | 北 | | | | | | | | |

| 街 | 丿 | 彳 | 彳 | 彳 | 彳 | 往 | 往 | 往 | 往 | 街 | 街 | | |

| 通 | 乛 | 乛 | 尸 | 丹 | 丹 | 甬 | 甬 | 诵 | 通 | | | | |

| 道 | 丶 | 丷 | 艹 | 艹 | 产 | 芦 | 芦 | 首 | 首 | 首 | 诮 | 道 | |

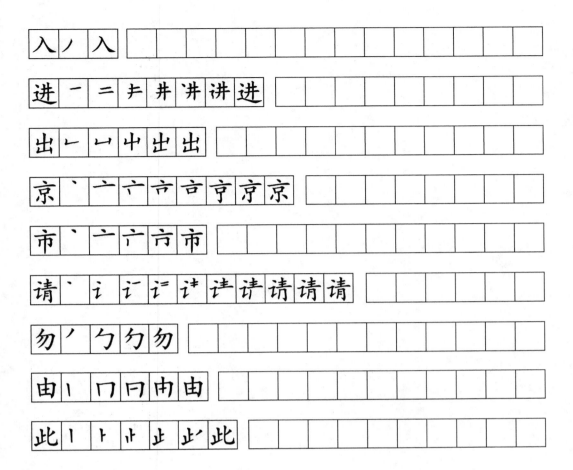

Writing Characters with Chinese Software

Write the following in Chinese characters using the Pinyin input method of your Chinese word-processing program. Alternatively, if you do not have access to a Chinese word-processing program, write out in handwriting the Pinyin with tones and the characters for each of these. The individual characters used in each of the following have been introduced in this lesson or a prior lesson.

1. east side of Beijing University
2. northwest corner
3. Western food
4. street-crossing passageway
5. entrance of the university
6. south gate of Nanjing
7. The United States is in North America.
8. Western Europe uses Euros.
9. import-export
10. Please go upstairs to the English Department.
11. The vegetable market is this way.
12. Please do not enter.
13. The ladies' room is 100 meters to the north.
14. book market entrance

15 Time (1)

第十五课　时间 (一)

Dì shíwǔ kè　*Shíjiān*

In this lesson you will learn to read and write sixteen Chinese characters related to signs and time.

The first four characters appear in many signs on the street and in tourist areas. The other twelve characters will help you read schedules in school, at work places, and elsewhere.

Sixteen Chinese characters that are related to signs and time
Four radicals
Structure of the characters
Practice reading character combinations
Practice reading signs
Practice reading sentences and a paragraph
Practice writing radicals and characters
Practice writing characters with Chinese word-processing software, using the Pinyin input method

NEW CHARACTERS

禁 jìn	to forbid; prohibition
止 zhǐ	to prohibit, to stop
步 bù	a step; to go on foot, to walk
内 nèi	inside, inner
早 zǎo	morning; early

午 wǔ	noon	
晚 wǎn	evening; late	
点 diǎn	o'clock; (decimal) point; to choose, to mark	
刻 kè	quarter of an hour; 15 minutes	
半 bàn	half, partly	
现 xiàn	now, present	
时 shí	time, the present time, hour	
开 kāi	to open; to set out; to turn on, to operate	
班 bān	class; shift; regularly-run	
休 xiū	to rest, to cease	
息 xī	to rest	

Business hours　　　Bike parking hours

LEARNING RADICALS

Learn these four radicals:

止	止	步	此	正
stop	zhǐ	bù	cǐ	zhèng
刂	刻	别	剃	刚
knife	kè	bié	tì	gāng
王	王	班	现	碧
king	wáng	bān	xiàn	bì
廾	开	弄	异	
folded arms	kāi	nòng	yì	

STRUCTURE OF THE CHARACTERS

Learn the radicals (R) and components of these sixteen Chinese characters:

禁	示 shì (reveal R) + 林 lín (woods); 林 = 木 mù (wood) + 木
止	止 zhǐ (step R)
步	止 zhǐ (step R)
内	冂 (borders R) + 人 rén (person)
早	日 rì (sun R) + 十 shí (ten)
午	𠂉 (R) + 十 shí (ten)
晚	日 rì (sun R) + 免 miǎn (dispense with); 免 = 𠂉 + 日 rì (sun) + 儿 ér (child)
点	灬 (four dots R) + 占 zhàn (occupy)
刻	刂 (knife R) + 亥 hài (the twelfth of the twelve Earthly Branches)
半	丨 (R) + 丷 + 二
现	王 (king R) + 见 jiàn (to see)
时	日 rì (sun R) + 寸 cùn (1/10 meter)
开	廾 (R) + 一

班	王 wáng (king R) + 乂 + 王
休	亻 (person R) + 木 mù (wood)
息	心 xīn (heart R) + 自 zì (self)

READING PRACTICE

1. Read the following words. These are compounds that combine a character from this lesson with other characters you have learned before. Don't memorize the meaning of those words. Try to analyze the meaning of each compound when you read, then look at the English translations given below to check if you get the correct meaning from the reading.

禁	禁地, 禁书
止	禁止, 禁止通行, 禁止过街, 禁止进入
步	步行, 步行街, 走步, 步子, 一步一步地
内	内外, 禁止入内, 内地, 内行, 内心, 内在, 三日内
早	早上, 早饭, 早餐, 早茶, 早班, 早市, 早晚, 早期
午	中午, 午饭, 午餐, 午休, 午前, 午后
晚	晚上, 晚饭, 晚餐, 晚班, 晚点, 晚间, 晚了
点	两点, 早点, 点心, 点菜, 点头, 一点儿, 上午十点, 早上十点晚上七点
刻	一刻, 三刻, 此刻
半	两点半, 一半, 半点, 半百, 半路, 半中半西, 半圆
现	现在, 现有, 现行, 现钱, 现学, 现学现教
时	时间, 午休时间, 上课时间, 下班时间, 上午九时, 学时 过时, 时刻, 时局, 时冷时热
开	开门, 开学, 开饭, 开水, 开办, 开市, 开门红, 开往, 开房间, 开茶馆, 开方子, 开口
班	上班, 下班, 三班, 头班, 下一班, 班子, 班房
休	休学, 午休, 休止
息	休息, 年息, 不息, 一息

English translations:

禁	禁地 forbidden area; 禁书 banned book
止	禁止 forbidden; 禁止通行 No Trespassing; 禁止过街 No Street Crossing; 禁止进入 Do Not Enter
步	步行 walk; 步行街 pedestrian street; 走步 walk with the ball (basketball); 步子 step, pace; 一步一步地 step by step
内	内外 domestic and foreign; 禁止入内 Do Not Enter; 内地 inland; 内行 expert; 内心 in one's heart; 内在 internal; 三日内 within three days
早	早上 morning; 早饭 breakfast; 早餐 breakfast; 早茶 "morning dim sum" (literally "morning tea," which has become a specific term for "breakfast" in Cantonese); 早班 morning shift; 早市 morning market; 早晚 morning and evening; 早期 early stage
午	中午 noon; 午饭 lunch; 午餐 lunch; 午休 noon break; 午前 morning; 午后 afternoon
晚	晚上 evening; 晚饭 dinner; 晚餐 dinner; 晚班 evening shift; 晚点 behind schedule; 晚间 in the evening; 晚了 late; 晚期 late stage

Business hours

点　两点 2:00; 早点 breakfast; 点心 dessert; 点菜 order dishes; 点头 nod one's head, OK; 一点儿 a little; 上午十点 10:00 A.M.; 早上六点 6:00 A.M.; 晚上七点 7:00 P.M.

刻　一刻 fifteen minutes; 三刻 forty-five minutes; 此刻 at the moment

半　两点半 2:30; 一半 half; 半点 the least bit; 半百 fifty years old; 半路 half way; 半中半西 half-Western half-Chinese; 半圆 half circle

现　现在 now; 现有 now available; 现行 currently in effect; 现钱 cash; 现学 pick up on the job; 现学现教 learn while teaching

时　时间 time; 午休时间 noon break time; 上课时间 class hour; 时刻 moment; 下班时间 off-work time; 上午九时 9:00 A.M.; 学时 credit-hour; 过时 out of date; 时局 the current political situation; 时冷时热 sometimes cold, sometimes hot

开　开门 open the door; 开学 school begins; 开饭 serve a meal; 开水 hot water; 开办 start; 开市 open for business; 开门红 make a good beginning; 开往 leave for; 开房间 get a hotel room; 开茶馆 operate a teahouse; 开方子 write a prescription; 开口 start to talk

班　上班 go to work; 下班 get off work; 三班 third class; 头班 first shift; 下一班 next scheduled (bus/train); 班子 organized group; 班房 jail

休　休学 stop school for a period of time; 午休 noon break; 休止 cease

息　休息 rest; 年息 annual interest; 不息 not stop; 一息 one breath

2. Read the following signs.

开门时间
早 8:00 – 下午 6:00

午休时间
中午 12:00 – 下午 2:00

现在休息

饮早茶请上二楼

禁止通行

人行横道

早点

烧饼

油条

油饼

炸鸡蛋

馒头

汤面

3. Read the following sentences.

a. 银行早上九点开门，晚上五点半关门。(关 guān, close)

b. 早上，上早班的人在马路边吃早点。

c. 中国有很多女人在早市买菜。

d. 晚上，很多人吃了晚饭上街走走。

e. 网吧的上网时间是早上六点到晚上十点。(到 dào, until)

f. 马路对面的小吃店卖西餐早点，有面包，牛奶和炸鸡蛋。

g. 小马开茶馆，小王开饭馆，小米开宾馆。

h. 中午午休时，我在饭馆吃饭。我吃了一个红烧鱼，一个素菜和米饭。一点一刻我去中国银行换人民币。中国银行中午休息，关门了。下午两点开门。我的汉语课是一点半上课，我去大学上汉语课了。三点下课。三点半我又去教英语。晚上我休息。

Chinese Radical Practice

1. Practice writing these radicals, using the correct stroke order.

止 _____

止 _____

刂 _____

刂 _____

王 _____

王 _____

卄 _____

卄 _____

2. In the lines below, write in characters from anywhere in this book that contain the radical given at the start of the row.

止 _____

刂 _____

王 _____

卄 _____

Chinese Character Practice

Practice writing the following characters by first tracing their outlines, and then writing them on your own. Follow the correct stroke order given here.

| 禁 | 一 | 十 | 才 | 木 | 木 | 村 | 村 | 林 | 林 | 埜 | 禁 | 禁 | 禁 | | | |

| 止 | 丨 | 卜 | 止 | 止 | | | | | | | | | | | | | | | | |

| 步 | 丶 | 丨 | 止 | 止 | 半 | 毕 | 步 | | | | | | | | | | | |

| 内 | 丨 | 冂 | 内 | 内 | | | | | | | | | | | | | | | |

| 早 | 丶 | 冂 | 曰 | 日 | 旦 | 早 | | | | | | | | | | | | |

| 午 | 丿 | 𠂉 | 仁 | 午 | | | | | | | | | | | | | | |

| 晚 | 丨 | 冂 | 日 | 日 | 日' | 旷 | 旷 | 晗 | 晗 | 晚 | 晚 | | | | | | |

| 点 | 丨 | 卜 | 上 | 占 | 占 | 占 | 点 | 点 | 点 | | | | | | | |

| 刻 | 丶 | 二 | 亠 | 亥 | 亥 | 亥 | 刻 | | | | | | | | | |

| 半 | 丶 | 丷 | 兰 | 兰 | 半 | | | | | | | | | | | | |

| 现 | 一 | 二 | 王 | 王 | 玑 | 玏 | 现 | 现 | | | | | | | | |

| 时 | 丨 | 冂 | 日 | 日 | 旷 | 时 | 时 | | | | | | | | | |

| 开 | 一 | 二 | 于 | 开 | | | | | | | | | | | | | |

| 班 | 一 | 二 | 三 | 王 | 王 | 玏 | 玪 | 玡 | 班 | 班 | | | | | | |

| 休 | 丿 | 亻 | 仁 | 什 | 休 | 休 | | | | | | | | | | |

| 息 | 丿 | 亻 | 冇 | 白 | 白 | 自 | 自 | 息 | 息 | 息 | | | | | | |

Writing Characters with Chinese Software

Write the following in Chinese characters using the Pinyin input method of your Chinese word-processing program. Alternatively, if you do not have access to a Chinese word-processing program, write out in handwriting the Pinyin with tones and the characters for each of these. The individual characters used in each of the following have been introduced in this lesson or a prior lesson.

1. no trespassing
2. do not enter
3. pedestrian street
4. no street crossing here
5. Dim sum is on the second floor.
6. The morning market is open from 6:00 to 9:30 A.M.
7. Miss Wang goes to lunch at the noon break.
8. The bus is behind schedule.
9. The annual interest is 5.2 percent.
10. half-Western half-Chinese
11. Little Wang ordered dishes for dinner. Little Ma nodded his head.
12. Little Qian learned Chinese while teaching English.
13. Little Ma gets off work at 5:00 P.M.
14. The Chinese class hour is 9:00–9:50 A.M.
15. Make your own list of breakfast foods.

Market hours

16 Time (2)

第十六课 时间 (二)

Dì shíliù kè　　　*Shíjiān*

In this lesson you will learn to read and write sixteen Chinese characters related to schedules.

Sixteen Chinese characters that are related to schedules
Four radicals
Structure of the characters
Practice reading character combinations
Practice reading signs and schedules
Practice reading a paragraph
Practice writing radicals and characters
Practice writing characters with Chinese word-processing software, using the Pinyin input method

NEW CHARACTERS

期 qī	period; to expect
作 zuò	to do, make; to act as; to write
表 biǎo	form, chart
汉 hàn	Chinese language
语 yǔ	words
课 kè	class, course
操 cāo	to operate; to exercise

第	(particle: indicates an ordinal number)
dì	
节	section, segment, period (of a class); festival, holiday
jié	
自	self; from
zì	
习	to practice, to be used to; habit
xí	
以	at, on, of, with, by; to use
yǐ	
营	to operate, to run; to seek
yíng	
业	trade, profession; estate
yè	
去	to go; away (after a verb, indicating action directed away from the speaker); past, previous
qù	
没	not; to not have (short form of 没有 méiyǒu)
méi	

LEARNING RADICALS

Learn these four radicals:

竹	竹	第	等	笔	笑
bamboo	zhú	dì	děng	bǐ	xiào
卩	卫	印			
seal	wèi	yìn			
自	自	息			
self	zì	xī			
殳	没	段	般		
lance	méi	duàn	bān		

Learn the radicals (R) and components of these sixteen Chinese characters:

期　月 yuè (moon R) + 其 qí (his)

作　亻 (person R) + 乍 zhà (first)

表　衣 yī (cloth R) + 龶

汉　氵 (water R) + 又 yòu (again)

语　讠 (word R) + 吾 wú (I, we); 吾 = 五 wǔ (five) + 口 kǒu (mouth)

课　讠 (word R) + 果 guǒ (fruit); 果 = 田 tián (field) + 木 mù (wood)

操　扌 (hand R) + 品 pǐn (product) + 木 mù (wood)

第　⺮ (bamboo R) + 弓 gōng (bow) + 丨 + 丿

节　艹 (grass R) + 卩

自　自 zì (self R) + 丿 + 目 mù (eye)

习　⁊ (R) + 冫

以　人 rén (person R) + ㇄ + 丶

营　艹 (grass R) + 冖 + 口 kǒu (mouth) + 口

业　业 yè (professions R) + 一

去　厶 (private R) + 土 tǔ (earth)

没　氵 (water R) + 殳 shū (an ancient weapon); 殳 = 几 jǐ (few) + 又 yòu (again)

READING PRACTICE

Read the following words. These are compounds that combine a character from this lesson with other characters you have learned before. Don't memorize the meaning of those words. Try to analyze the meaning of each compound when you read, then look at the English translations given below to check if you get the correct meaning from the reading.

期　学期, 上学期, 下学期, 期中, 期间, 期货, 到期, 一期

作　作息, 作息时间, 作文, 作出, 作用, 作对, 作乐

表	表白 表面, 表现, 时间表, 表面上, 表里不一
汉	汉人, 汉学, 汉子, 汉水, 大汉, 老汉
语	汉语, 英语, 外语, 语文, 语系
课	上课, 下课, 课间, 课外, 课时, 汉语课
操	作操, 早操, 课间操 操作
第	第一, 第一名, 第一节, 第一学期, 第五课, 第七街 第十个, 第三国
节	节日, 时节, 过节, 节电, 节目, 节节, 一节课
自	自从, 自学, 自由, 自大, 自白, 自转, 自食其力
习	自习, 习作
以	以前, 以后, 以上, 以下, 以内, 以外, 以此, 以往
营	营业, 国营, 营地, 营房
业	作业, 学业, 行业, 饮食业
去	去路, 去年, 去过, 去过中国, 去教室, 去电话
没	没有, 没人, 没课, 没门儿, 没出路, 没大没小, 没去上课, 去过中国, 没有, 没去过

English translations:

期	学期 semester; 上学期 last semester; 下学期 next semester; 期中 midterm; 期间 period; 期货 commodity futures; 到期 due time; 一期 one phase
作	作息 work and rest; 作息时间 daily schedule; 作文 composition; 作出 make out; 作用 affect; 作对 oppose; 作乐 have a good time
表	表白 explain oneself; 表面 surface; 表现 display; 时间表 time table; 表面上 on the surface of; 表里不一 think in one way and act another
汉	汉人 Chinese; 汉学 Sinology; 汉子 man; 汉水 Han river; 大汉 big fellow; 老汉 old man

语	汉语 Chinese language; 英语 English language; 外语 foreign language; 语文 language and literature; 语系 language family
课	上课 go to class; 下课 finish class; 课间 class break; 课外 outside of class, extracurricular; 课时 class hour; 汉语课 Chinese class
操	作操 do exercises; 早操 morning exercises; 课间操 class-break exercises; 操作 to operate
第	第一 number one, first; 第一名 first place; 第一节 first class period; 第一学期 first semester; 第五课 Lesson Five; 第七街 Seventh Avenue; 第十个 number ten, tenth; 第三国 a third country
节	节日 holiday; 时节 season; 过节 celebrate holidays; 节电 save electricity; 节目 program; 节节 successively; 一节课 one class
自	自从 since; 自学 study independently; 自由 freedom; 自大 arrogant; 自白 confession; 自转 rotation; 自食其力 self-support
习	自习 (time for) individual study; 习作 do exercises in compositions
以	以前 before; 以后 later; 以上 above; 以下 below; 以内 within; 以外 beyond; 以此 for this reason; 以往 previous
营	营业 do business; 国营 state-run; 营地 campsite; 营房 barracks
业	作业 homework, operation; 学业 course of study; 行业 line of business; 饮食业 catering trade
去	去路 the way along which one is going; 去年 last year; 去过 have been to; 去过中国 have been to China; 去教室 go to the classroom; 去电话 call up
没	没有 not have; 没人 nobody; 没课 no class; 没门儿 have no way of doing something; 没出路 no way out; 没大没小 show no respect to a senior; 没去上课 didn't go to class; 去过中国没有 Have you been to China?; 没去过 never been to

2. Read the following signs.

第四教学楼

英语系办公室在楼上

国营商店

澡堂

营房

禁止入内

营业时间
上午: 8:00–12:00
下午: 2:00–5:00
休息时间: 中午 12:00–2:00

3. Read the following daily schedule.

第一学期作息时间表

上午	早操	6:20–6:40
早餐		6:40–7:10
第一节	汉语	7:30–8:10
第二节	英语	8:20–9:00
第三节	电脑 (diànnǎo, computer)	9:10–9:50
课间操		9:50–10:15
第四节	数学	10:15–10:55
眼保健操 (yǎn, eyes; bǎojiàn, healthcare)	11:05–11:10	
第五节	历史 (lìshǐ, history)	11:10–11:50
午餐	11:50–12:20	

Success with Chinese: Reading & Writing

下午	午休	12:20–1:50
第六节	中国文学	2:00–2:40
第七节	英美文学	2:50–3:30
第八节	地理 (dìlǐ, geography)	3:40–4:20
课外活动 (huódòng, activity)	4:30–5:30	
晚上	晚餐	5:30
自习	6:45–8:00	
休息	8:00–9:30	

4. Read the following paragraph.

早上我六点半起床。起床以后我洗澡。我在外边吃早点。我七点三刻去大学，八点在中文系上汉语课。十点下课。下课以后我去英语系教英语，我的班上有十个学生。十二点五十分下英语课，我和学生一起去饭馆吃午饭。吃饭以后我上街走走。中午商店都关门了，我去学校大门旁边的网吧上网。下午我上英美文学课。晚上我没有作业。我十点睡觉。早睡早起。

WRITING PRACTICE

Chinese Radical Practice

1. Practice writing these radicals, using the correct stroke order.

ⵓⵓ _____

ⵓⵓ _____

卩 _____

卩 _____

自 _____

自 _____

殳 _____

殳 _____

2. In the lines below, write in characters from anywhere in this book that contain the radical given at the start of the row.

竹 _____

卩 _____

自 _____

殳 _____

Chinese Character Practice

Practice writing the following characters by first tracing their outlines, and then writing them on your own. Follow the correct stroke order given here.

期	一	十	卄	廿	甘	其	其	其	期	期	期	期				

作	ノ	亻	亻	作	竹	作	作									

表	一	二	丰	圭	声	耒	表	表								

汉	丶	冫	氵	汈	汉											

语	丶	讠	讠	讦	诌	语	语	语	语							

课	丶	讠	讠	讱	讵	讵	诨	课	课	课						

操	一	扌	扌	扩	护	护	护	护	操	操	操	操	操	操
第	ノ	ト	ド	竹	竹	竹	竺	笃	笃	第	第			
节	一	一	艹	艻	节									
自	ノ	亻	白	白	白	自								
习	丁	习	习											
以	丶	丷	以	以										
营	一	一	艹	艹	芦	节	带	营	营	营				
业	丨	丨丨	业	业	业									
去	一	十	土	去	去									
没	丶	冫	氵	氵	氿	没	没							

Writing Characters with Chinese Software

Write the following in Chinese characters using the Pinyin input method of your Chinese word-processing program. Alternatively, if you do not have access to a Chinese word-processing program, write out in handwriting the Pinyin with tones and the characters for each of these. The individual characters used in each of the following have been introduced in this lesson or a prior lesson.

1. I have a midterm this morning.
2. The homework is due today.
3. The bank's business hours are 9:00–5:00.
4. This semester has two holidays.
5. Please save electricity.
6. The third period class is a Chinese language class.

7. Miss Ma has been in the United States before.

8. Miss Qian exchanged money after class.

9. Seventh Avenue is the next street.

10. He is number one in the class.

11. Catering is a good business.

12. Little Wang shows no respect to a senior.

13. He did not go to class this afternoon.

14. After dinner is the self-study period.

15. Make a timetable of your daily schedule.

17

Calendars

第十七课　日历

Dì shíqī kè   *Rìlì*

In this lesson you will learn to read and write sixteen Chinese characters related to schedules and calendars.

Sixteen Chinese characters that are related to schedules and calendars
Four radicals
Structure of the characters
Practice reading character combinations
Practice reading calendars and dates
Practice reading signs and announcements
Practice writing radicals and characters
Practice writing characters with Chinese word-processing software,
     using the Pinyin input method

NEW CHARACTERS

星 xīng	star; a bit
天 tiān	day
年 nián	year
周 zhōu	week; cycle
末 mò	end; powder; last
今 jīn	the present, today
明 míng	tomorrow, next; bright

昨	yesterday, past
zuó	
每	every, each
měi	
正	first (in lunar calendar); upright; main
zhēng/zhèng	
初	beginning, elementary
chū	
春	spring
chūn	
新	new
xīn	
寒	cold
hán	
暑	heat, hot weather
shǔ	
假	false; holiday, vacation
jiǎ/jià	

LEARNING RADICALS

Learn these four radicals:

人 **person**	人 rén	今 jīn	个 gè	入 rù	以 yǐ	
母 **mother**	母 mǔ	每 měi	毋 wú			
衤 **clothes**	初 chū	衬 chèn	衫 shān	裤 kù	袜 wà	裙 qún
斤 **axe**	斤 jīn	新 xīn	所 suǒ			

STRUCTURE OF THE CHARACTERS

Learn the radicals (R) and components of these sixteen Chinese characters:

星	日 rì (sun R) + 生 shēng (life)
天	一 yī (one R) + 大 dà (big)
年	宀 (R)
周	冂 (border R) + 土 tǔ (earth) + 口 kǒu (mouth)
末	一 yī (one R) + 木 mù (wood)
今	人 rén (person R)
明	日 rì (sun R) + 月 yuè (moon)
昨	日 rì (sun R) + 乍 zhà (first)
每	母 mǔ (mother R) + 宀
正	一 yī (one R) + 止 zhǐ (stop)
初	衤 (clothes R) + 刀 dāo (knife)
春	日 rì (sun R) + 夫 (chūn head)
新	斤 jīn (axe R) + 亲 qīn (relative)
寒	宀 (roof R)
暑	日 rì (sun R) + 者 zhě (-er)
假	亻 (person R)

READING PRACTICE

Read the following words. These are compounds that combine a character from this lesson with other characters you have learned before. Don't memorize the meaning of those words. Try to analyze the meaning of each compound when you read, then look at the English translations given below to check if you get the correct meaning from the reading.

星	星期, 星期一, 星期二, 星期三, 星期四, 星期五, 星期六 星期日
天	星期天, 天天, 一天, 明天, 天明, 天边, 天地, 天上天文学, 天下, 天下第一

年	去年，年头，年度，年末，年节，年年，过年，老年，一年
周	周末，周日，周五，周年，周期，周转，一周
末	末年，末期，末班，末了，末日
今	今天，今日，今年，今晚，今后，今人
明	明天，明年，明晚，明日，明白，明月，明星
昨	昨天，昨晚，昨日
每	每天，每星期，每周，每月，每年，每日，每小时，每人
正	正月，正午，正点，正好，正门，正面，正文，正在，正中
初	年初，正月初一，初春，初冬，初期，初小，初中
春	春天，春日，春节，春假，春饼，春寒，春末
新	新年，新月，新人，新房，新书，新路子，新局面，新星
寒	寒假，寒冷，寒风，寒酸，寒毛
暑	暑假，暑期，暑天，中暑
假	假日，假期，假条，请假

English translations:

星	星期 week; 星期一 Monday; 星期二 Tuesday; 星期三 Wednesday; 星期四 Thursday; 星期五 Friday; 星期六 Saturday; 星期日 Sunday
天	星期天 Sunday; 天天 everyday; 一天 one day; 明天 tomorrow; 天明 dawn; 天边 horizon; 天地 heaven and earth; 天上 the sky; 天文学 astronomy; 天下 the world, land under heaven; 天下第一 number one in the world

年　去年 last year; 年头 year; 年度 fiscal year; 年末 end of the year;
年节 New Year holiday; 年年 year after year; 过年 celebrate New Year;
老年 old year; 一年 one year

周　周末 weekend; 周 week; 周五 Friday; 周年 anniversary;
周期 cycle; 周转 turnover; 一周 one week

末　末年 end of a dynasty; 末期 last phase; 末班 last bus (or train);
末了 finally; 末日 doomsday

今　今天 today; 今日 today, now; 今年 this year; 今晚 tonight;
今后 from now on; 今人 moderns, contemporaries

明　明天 tomorrow; 明年 next year; 明晚 tomorrow night;
明日 tomorrow; 明白 understand; 明月 bright moon; 明星 stars

昨　昨天 yesterday; 昨晚 last night; 昨日 yesterday

每　每天 everyday; 每星期 every week; 每周 every week;
每月 every month; 每年 every year; 每 every day; 每小时 every hour;
每人 every person

正　正月 first month; 正午 high noon; 正点 on time; 正好 just right;
正门 front door; 正面 facade; 正文 main text; 正在 is doing;
正中 center, hit the target

初　年初 beginning of the year; 正月初一 first day of the first month (lunar
year); 初春 early spring; 初冬 early winter; 初期 initial stage;
初小 elementary school; 初中 junior high school

春　春天 spring; 春日 spring days; 春节 Spring Festival; 春假 Spring break;
春饼 spring pancake; 春寒 spring chill; 春末 end of spring

新　新年 New Year; 新月 crescent moon; 新人 newlywed; 新房 bridal
chamber; 新书 new book; 新路子 new approach; 新局面 new
situation; 新星 new star

寒　寒假 winter vacation; 寒冷 cold; 寒风 cold wind; 寒酸 shabby and
miserable; 寒毛 fine body hair

暑　暑假 summer vacation; 暑期 summer term; 暑天 hot summer day;
　中暑 suffer sunstroke

假　假日 holiday; 假期 day off; 假条 leave permit; 请假 ask for a leave of
　absence

2. Read the following Chinese calendars.

二〇〇四年
星期天
十二月大
初六
二十三小寒

3. Read the following days, months, and years.

一月，二月，三月，四月，五月，六月
七月，八月，九月，十月，十一月，十二月
一七七四年七月四日，一九一一年十月十日
一九四九年十月一日，二零零四年九月一日

4. Read the following signs.

新年快乐

春节快乐

5. Read the following announcements.

这个月每星期五下午上一节课（两点到三点）。
今年新年放假一天，加上星期六和星期日共三天假。春
节放假五天。寒假从二月三号到三月一号。
假期中学校图书馆不开门。

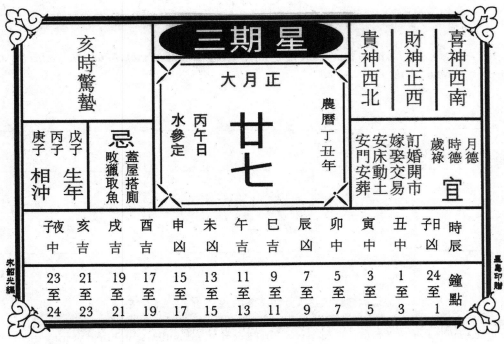

A lunar calendar

WRITING PRACTICE

Chinese Radical Practice

1. Practice writing these radicals, using the correct stroke order.

人 _____

人 _____

母 _____

母 _____

衤 _____

衤 _____

斤 _____

斤 _____

2. In the lines below, write in characters from anywhere in this book that contain the radical given at the start of the row.

人 _____

母 _____

衤 _____

斤 _____

Chinese Character Practice

Practice writing the following characters by first tracing their outlines, and then writing them on your own. Follow the correct stroke order given here.

星	丶	冂	冂	日	尸	星	星	旱	星							

天	一	二	于	天											

年	丿	宀	丷	乞	仁	三	年								

周	丿	冂	月	円	用	用	周	周							

末	一	二	十	才	末											

Writing Characters with Chinese Software

Write the following in Chinese characters using the Pinyin input method of your Chinese word-processing program. Alternatively, if you do not have access to a Chinese word-processing program, write out in handwriting the Pinyin with tones and the characters for each of these. The individual characters used in each of the following have been introduced in this lesson or a prior lesson.

1. The first day of the first month (of the lunar year) is Spring Festival.
2. The winter vacation is from December 19 to January 15.
3. Summer is very hot in Beijing.
4. Little Wang is going to China during the spring break.

5. Happy New Year!

6. On weekends, Miss Ma does laundry on Saturday and rests on Sunday.

7. The American went to China last year.

8. Tonight and tomorrow night there will be a bright moon.

9. Every day of the winter break is cold.

10. Spring break is a one-week vacation.

11. Chinese celebrate Spring Festival.

12. The old man was at the front gate yesterday in the chill wind.

13. Miss Wang is number one in the class every year.

14. Today is September 18, 2004.

15. July 4 is American Independence Day.

18

Filling in Forms

第十八课　填表

Dì shíbā kè　　*Tiánbiǎo*

In this lesson you will learn to read and write eighteen Chinese characters related to filling in various official forms.

Eighteen Chinese characters that are related to filling in various official forms

Four radicals

Structure of the characters

Practice reading character combinations related to filling in official forms

Practice reading signs

Practice filling in forms

Practice reading a long sentence

Writing practice for radicals and characters

Practice writing characters with Chinese word-processing software, using the Pinyin input method

NEW CHARACTERS

姓 xìng	to be surnamed; surname, family name
名 míng	name; fame
性 xìng	sex; nature; gender
别 bié	difference; don't
龄 líng	age, duration
职 zhí	job, position

生 shēng	to give birth to, to be born to, to grow, life; raw
校 xiào	school work; worker; skill
工 gōng	work; worker; skill
位 wèi	place; position
址 zhǐ	location, site
婚 hūn	marriage; to wed
姻 yīn	marriage; in-law
境 jìng	border, territory, condition
护 hù	to guard, to protect

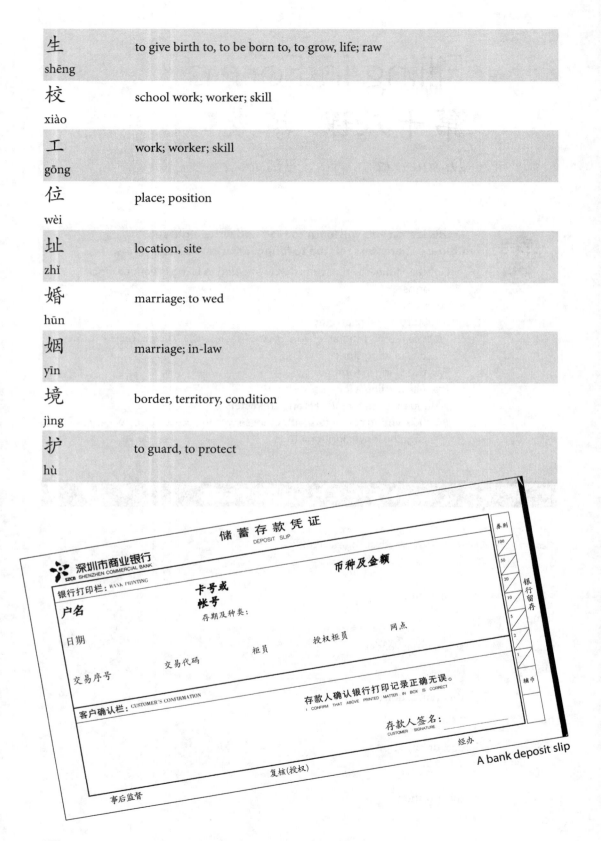

A bank deposit slip

Success with Chinese: Reading & Writing

照	to photograph; license
zhào	
签	to sign; label
qiān	
证	certification, proof; to prove
zhēng/zhèng	

LEARNING RADICALS

Learn these four radicals:

忄	性	忙	快	慢
heart	xìng	máng	kuài	màn
齿	齿	龄	龈	
tooth	chǐ	líng	yín	
耳	耳	职	聊	
ear	ěr	zhí	liáo	
立	立	站	亲	产
stand	lì	zhàn	qīn	chǎn

STRUCTURE OF THE CHARACTERS

Learn the radicals (R) and components of these eighteen Chinese characters:

姓	女 nǚ (woman R) + 生 shēng (birth)
名	夕 xí (sunset R) + 口 kǒu (mouth)
性	忄 (heart R) + 生 shēng (birth)
别	刂 (knife R) + 另 lìng (other); 另 = 口 kǒu (mouth) + 力 lì (power)
龄	齿 chǐ (tooth R) + 令 ling (order)
职	耳 ěr (ear R) + 只 zhí (only); 只 = 口 kǒu (mouth) + 八 bā (eight)
生	丿 (left-falling stroke R)

Lesson 18: Filling in Forms

校	木 mù (wood R) + 交 jiāo (hand over)
工	工 gōng (work R)
位	亻 (person R) + 立 lì (stand)
址	土 tǔ (earth R) + 止 zhǐ (to see)
婚	女 nǚ (woman R) + 昏 hūn (dusk); 昏 = 氏 shì (surname) + 日 rì (sun)
姻	女 nǚ (woman R) + 因 yīn (reason)
境	土 tǔ (earth R) + 竟 jìng (finish); 竟 = 立 lì (stand) + 日 rì (sun) + 儿 ér (son)
护	扌 (hand R) + 户 hù (household)
照	灬 (four dots R) + 日 rì (sun) + 召 zhāo (to call);
	召 = 刀 dāo (knife) + 口 kǒu (mouth)
签	竹 (bamboo R) + 金 qiǎn (wood)
证	讠 (word R) + 正 zhèng (straight)

READING PRACTICE

1. Read the following words. These are compounds that combine a character from this lesson with other characters you have learned before. Don't memorize the meaning of those words. Try to analyze the meaning of each compound when you read, then look at the English translations given below to check if you get the correct meaning from the reading.

姓	姓氏, 姓王, 姓马
名	姓名, 名片, 名单, 名酒, 名人, 名校, 地名
性	女性, 男性, 性子
别	性别, 别人, 别去, 别走
龄	年龄, 学龄
职	职业, 职位, 职员, 在职
生	学生, 生日, 师生, 人生, 生手, 生人, 生菜, 生肉 花生 一生
校	校名, 学校, 校办, 校外
工	工作, 工人, 工龄, 工厂, 工钱, 工业, 工商业

位	职位, 位子, 两位, 第十位, 个位
址	地址, 校址, 厂址
婚	婚龄 婚期
姻	婚姻
境	入境, 出境, 国境, 边境, 境地
护	护理, 护路, 护面
照	护照, 照片, 照办, 照料, 照面, 照明
签	签名, 签到, 书签
证	签证, 工作证, 出生证, 证人, 证书, 证明, 证婚人

English translations:

姓	姓氏 surname; 姓王 surname is Wang; 姓马 surname is Ma
名	姓名 full name; 名片 name card; 名单 roster; 名酒 vintage wine; 名人 celebrity; 名校 famous school; 地名 place name
性	女性 female; 男性 male; 性子 temper
别	性别 sex, gender; 别人 others; 别去 do not go; 别走 do not leave
龄	年龄 age; 学龄 school-age
职	职业 profession; 职位 position; 职员 staff; 在职 at one's post
生	学生 student; 生日 birthday; 师生 student-teacher; 人生 life; 生手 new to a job; 生人 stranger; 生菜 lettuce; 生肉 raw meat; 花生 peanut; 一生 one's lifetime
校	校名 name of the school; 学校 school; 校办 school-run; 校外 outside of school
工	工作 work; 工人 worker; 工龄 length of service; 工厂 factory; 工钱 wages; 工业 industry; 工商业 industrial and commercial circles
位	职位 position; 位子 seat; 第十位 number ten; 个位 units place; 两位 two people
址	地址 address; 校址 school address; 厂址 factory address

婚	婚龄 marriageable age; 婚期 wedding date
姻	婚姻 marriage
境	入境 enter a country; 出境 leave the country; 国境 national boundary; 边境 border; 境地 condition
护	护理 nurse; 护路 road maintenance; 护面 mask
照	护照 passport; 照片 picture; 照办 act upon; 照料 take care of; 照面儿 show up; 照明 illumination
签	签名 sign; 签到 sign in; 书签 bookmark
证	签证 visa; 工作证 employee ID card; 出生证 birth certificate; 证人 witness; 证书 certification; 证明 prove; 证婚人 chief witness at a wedding ceremony

2. Read the following signs.

入境签证处

外宾入境处

护照照片

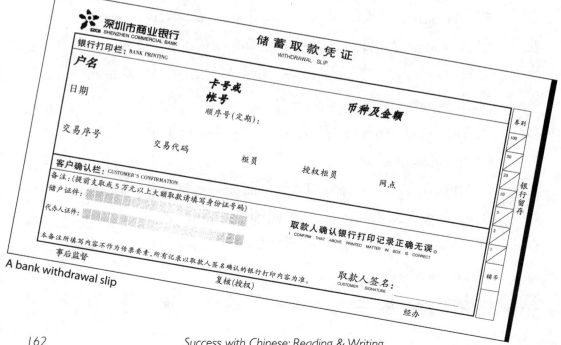

A bank withdrawal slip

由此出境

校办工厂

商学院

在此办理工作证

教师休息室

3. Fill in the following forms.

学生入学申请表

姓名 _____ 年龄 _____

国家 _____

学校 _____

学系 _____

学年 _____

进校时间 _____

门诊病卡 (Ménzhěn bìnglì kǎ–Medical Record)

姓名 _____ 性别 _____ 年龄 _____

职业 _____

婚姻: 已 (yǐ, married) _____ 未 (wèi, not married) _____

地址 _____

医院地址 (yīyuàn, hospital) _____

邮编 (biān, code) _____

急诊电话 (jízhěn, emergency): _____

4. Read the following sentence.

入境表上有姓名，性别，生日，年龄，婚姻，工作单位，职业，地址，在中国要去的地方，护照上的签证日期，签证地点和出境时间。不用照片。

WRITING PRACTICE

Chinese Radical Practice

1. Practice writing these radicals, using the correct stroke order.

忄 _____

忄 _____

齿 _____

齿 _____

耳 _____

耳 _____

立 _____

立 _____

2. In the lines below, write in characters from anywhere in this book that contain the radical given at the start of the row.

忄 _____

齿 _____

耳 _____

立 _____

Chinese Character Practice

Practice writing the following characters by first tracing their outlines, and then writing them on your own. Follow the correct stroke order given here.

姓	く	女	女	女	姓	姓	姓	姓

名 ´ ク 夕 夕 名 名

性 ` ` 忄 忄 忙 忙 性 性

别 ` 冖 口 号 另 别 别

龄 ⌐ ⊦ ⊦ 止 齿 齿 齿 齿 龄 龄 龄 龄

职 一 ⌐ ⊓ 丌 丌 耳 耵 职 职 职 职

生 ´ ㇒ ㇑ 牛 生

校 一 ㇒ ㇑ 木 术 杧 杧 杧 杧 校

工 一 丁 工

位 ノ 亻 亻 位 位 位 位

址 一 ㇒ 土 圠 圵 址 址

婚 く 女 女 女 妒 妒 姁 姁 婚 婚

姻 く 女 女 圽 姻 姻 姻 姻

境 一 ⊦ 土 圹 圹 圹 圹 垃 垃 境 墇 境

护 一 ㇒ 扌 护 护 护 护

Writing Characters with Chinese Software

Write the following in Chinese characters using the Pinyin input method of your Chinese word-processing program. Alternatively, if you do not have access to a Chinese word-processing program, write out in handwriting the Pinyin with tones and the characters for each of these. The individual characters used in each of the following have been introduced in this lesson or a prior lesson.

1. The Chinese student's name is Wang Ming.
2. Beijing University and Nanjing University are both famous schools.
3. Please sign your name on this form.
4. My name, age, address and visa are on the passport.
5. Sign in at 8:00 A.M.
6. Miss Qian's name card has her position, address, and phone number.
7. Don't leave. Please leave after dinner.
8. Today is an American student's birthday. Teachers and students are having dinner to celebrate.
9. Wang works at a factory.
10. two people
11. The school name is Nanjing University.
12. There are two genders: female and male.
13. Lettuce can be eaten, but not raw meat.
14. Passports and employee ID cards all have a picture.
15. Miss Ma's profession is "office staff."

 # Appendix I

Radical List by Lesson

LESSON 2

口	四	圆	国
enclosure	sì	yuán	guó
儿	儿	元	兑
child	ér	yuán	duì
白	白	百	的
white	bái	bǎi	de
亠	六	京	旁
cover	liù	jīng	páng

LESSON 3

土	土	块	在	坐
earth	tǔ	kuài	zài	zuò
刀丷⺈	刀	分	奂	角
knife	dāo	fēn	huàn	jiǎo
钅	钱	银	钞	钟
metal	qián	yín	chāo	zhōng
夕	夕	外	多	名
sunset	xí	wài	duō	míng

彳	行	很	往	街
step	háng/xíng	hěn	wǎng/wàng	jiē

扌	拌	换	打	拨
hand	bàn	huàn	dǎ	bō

欠	欠	欧	次	欢
owe	qiàn	ōu	cì	huān

厶	台	去	叁	能
private	tái	qù	sān	néng

LESSON 5

饣	饭	馆	馒	饼	饺	饮
food	fàn	guǎn	mán	bǐng	jiǎo	yǐn

艹	菜	茶	蒸	葱	茄	英
grass	cài	chá	zhēng	cōng	qié	yīng

氵	汤	清	滑	溜
water	tāng	qīng	huá	liū

虫	虫	虾	蛋
insect	cóng	xiā	dàn

LESSON 6

火	烧	炒	爆	炸
fire	shāo	chǎo	bào	zhá

灬	蒸
four dots	zhēng

米	料	糖
rice	liào	táng

酉			酸	酱	醋
yǒu (the tenth of the twelve Earthly Branches)			suān	jiàng	cù

纟	丝	红	绿	给		
silk	sī	hóng	lǜ	gěi		
广	广	腐	唐	店	床	麻
broad	guǎng	fǔ	táng	diàn	chuáng	má
鸟	鸟	鸭	鸡	鹅	鸽	
bird	niǎo	yā	jī	é	gē	
心	葱	您	怎	息		
heart	cōng	nín	zěn	xī		

口	口	咖	啡	可	啤	吃	喝
mouth	kǒu	kā	fēi	kě	pí	chī	hē
木	条	杯	桔	橘	床	果	棍
wood	tiáo	bēi	jú	jú	chuáng	guǒ	gùn
小	少	尘	尔	尝			
small	shǎo	chén	ěr	cháng			
女	女	奶	好	姐	要	她	婆
female	nǚ	nǎi	hǎo	jiě	yào	tā	pó

冫	冷	冰	次	准
ice	lěng	bīng	cì	zhǔn
禾	禾	香	和	秋
grain	hé	xiāng	hé	qiū
日	日	早	晚	春
sun	rì	zǎo	wǎn	chūn
冂	肉	网	同	
borders	ròu	wǎng	tóng	

LESSON 10

讠	话	请	谢	谁	语		
word	huà	qǐng	xiè	shéi	yǔ		

阝	邮	都	那	哪	附		
ear (left/right)	yóu	dōu	nà	nǎ	fù		

尸	尸	局	尺	屋	层		
corpse	shī	jú	chǐ	wū	céng		

乛	买	也					
	mǎi	yě					

月	月	有	服	肝	肥	肠	肺
moon	yuè	yǒu	fú	gān	féi	cháng	fèi

LESSON 11

方	方	房	旁	旅			
square	fāng	fáng	páng	lǚ			

门	门	间	问	们			
door	mén	jiān	wèn	mén			

宀	宾	客	室	字			
roof	bīn	kè	shì	zì			

厂	厂	厕	厅	厨	历	厉	
factory	chǎng	cè	tīng	chú	lì	lì	

LESSON 12

又	又	对	双	友	难				
also	yòu	duì	shuāng	yǒu	nán				

工	工	左	差	功					
work	gōng	zuǒ	chā	gōng					

辶	边	过	通	道	近	进	这	还	送
walk	biān	guò	tōng	dào	jìn	jìn	zhè	huái	sòng

𧾷	足	路	跟						
foot	zú	lù	gēn						

LESSON 13

攵	教	数	修	各
literature	jiāo	shù	xiū	gè
子 / 孑	子	学	孩	字
child	zǐ	xué	hái	zì
力	力	办	加	男
power	lì	bàn	jiā	nán
卜	卜	卡	外	占
divination	bǔ	kǎ	wài	zhàn

LESSON 14

匕	匕	北	比	化
spoon	bǐ	běi	bǐ	huà
亻	你	他	们	什
man	nǐ	tā	mén	shén
巾	巾	市	币	
towel	jīn	shì	bì	
勹	勿	勺	包	句
wrap	wù	sháo	bāo	jù

LESSON 15

止	止	步	此	正
stop	zhǐ	bù	cǐ	zhèng
刂	刻	别	剃	刚
knife	kè	bié	tì	gāng
王	王	班	现	碧
king	wáng	bān	xiàn	bì
廾	开	弄	异	
folded-arms	kāi	nòng	yì	

LESSON 16

𥫕	竹	第	等	笔	笑
bamboo	zhú	dì	děng	bǐ	xiào

卩	卫	印
seal	wèi	yìn

自	自	息
self	zì	xī

殳	没	段	般
lance	méi	duàn	bān

LESSON 17

母	母	每	毋
mother	mǔ	měi	wú

衤	初	衬	衫	裤	袜	裙
clothes	chū	chèn	shān	kù	wà	qún

斤	斤	新	所
axe	jīn	xīn	suǒ

LESSON 18

忄	性	忙	快	慢
heart	xìng	máng	kuài	màn

齿	齿	龄	龈
tooth	chǐ	líng	yín

耳	耳	职	聊
ear	ěr	zhí	liáo

立	立	站	亲	产
stand	lì	zhàn	qīn	chǎn

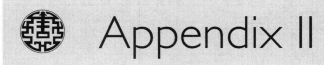

Appendix II

List of Radicals

	One Stroke		24	八 (丷) eight		48	工 work
1	丶 dot		25	乂		49	土 (士)
2	一 one		26	勹 wrap		50	艹 grass
3	丨		27	刀 (刁) knife		51	廾 folded hands
4	丿		28	力 power		52	大 big
5	乁		29	儿 boy		53	尢 crooked
6	乛		30	几 table		54	寸 inch
7	乙 (乀乚)		31	マ		55	扌 hand
	Two Strokes		32	卩 seal		56	弋 a dart
8	冫 ice		33	阝 (left-ear)		57	巾 kerchief
9	亠 cover		34	阝 (right-ear)		58	口 mouth
10	讠 word		35	又 again		59	囗 enclosure
11	二 two		36	辵 walk		60	山 mountain
12	十 ten		37	厶 private		61	屮 sprout
13	厂 plant		38	凵 receptacle		62	彳 step
14	ナ zuǒ-head		39	匕 spoon		63	彡 long hairs
15	匚 basket			Three Strokes		64	夕 evening
16	卜 to divine		40	氵 water		65	夂 from back
17	刂 knife		41	忄 (小) heart		66	丸 ball
18	冖 to cover		42	爿 (丬)		67	尸 corpse
19	冂 borders		43	亡 die		68	飠 (食) food
20	勹		44	广 broad		69	犭 dog
21	亻 man		45	宀 roof		70	彐
22	厂		46	门 door		71	弓
23	人 person		47	辶 walk		72	女 female

73	巳 (巳) self	104	曰 say	135	甘 sweet
74	子 (孑) child	105	中 center	136	石 stone
75	马 horse	106	贝 cowry	137	龙 dragon
76	幺 small	107	见 see	138	戊
77	纟 (糸) silk	108	父 father	139	⺌
78	巛	109	气 air	140	业 profession
79	小 (⺍) little	110	牛(牛) cow	141	目 eye

	Four Strokes	111	手 hand	142	田 land
80	⺍ four dots	112	毛 hair	143	由 cause
81	心 heart	113	攵 literary	144	申 state
82	斗 peck	114	片 strip	145	⺲ net
83	火 fire	115	斤 axe	146	皿 dish
84	文 literature	116	爪 (⺥) claws	147	钅 metal
85	方 square	117	尺 ruler	148	矢 arrow
86	礻 reveal	118	月 moon	149	禾 grain
87	户 household	119	殳 lance	150	白 white
88	王 king	120	欠 owe	151	瓜 melon
89	主	121	风 wind	152	鸟 bird
90	夭 (天) early	122	氏 surname	153	皮 skin
91	韦 leather	123	比 compare	154	癶
92	老	124	聿 stylus	155	矛 lance
93	廿 (卄)	125	水 water	156	疋 cloth
94	木 wood		**Five Strokes**		**Six Strokes**
95	不 not	126	立 stand	157	羊 (⺶ ⺷) sheep
96	犬 dog	127	疒 sickness	158	关
97	歹 bad	128	穴 cave	159	米 rice
98	瓦 tile	129	衤 clothes	160	齐 neat
99	牙 teeth	130	夫	161	衣 clothes
100	车 vehicle	131	玉 jade	162	亦 also
101	戈 spear	132	示 reveal	163	耳 ear
102	止 stop	133	去 go	164	臣 minister
103	日 sun	134	营	165	戋

166	西（覀）west	189	走 walk	Nine Strokes	
167	棘	190	赤 red	211	音 sound
168	亞 second	191	豆 bean	212	革 rawhide
169	而 but	192	束 bind	213	是 yes
170	頁 head	193	酉	214	骨 bone
171	至 to	194	豖 pig	215	香 fragrant
172	光 light	195	里 inside	216	鬼 ghost
173	庀 tiger	196	足 foot	217	食 eat
174	虫 insect	197	采 pick	Ten Strokes	
175	缶 clay pot	198	豸 reptile	218	高 high
176	耒 plough	199	谷 valley	219	鬲
177	舌 tongue	200	身 body	220	髟 hair
178	竹 bamboo	201	角 horn	Eleven Strokes	
179	臼 mortar	Eight Strokes		221	麻 hemp
180	自 self	202	青 blue	222	鹿 deer
181	血 blood	203	卓	Twelve Strokes	
182	舟 boat	204	雨 rain	223	黑 black
183	羽 feather	205	非 not	Thirteen Strokes	
184	艮 perverse	206	齒 tooth	224	鼓 drum
Seven Strokes		207	黽 toad	225	鼠 rat
185	言 word	208	隹 bird	Fourteen Strokes	
186	辛 bitter	209	金 gold	226	鼻 nose
187	辰 hour	210	魚 fish	227	others
188	麦 wheat				

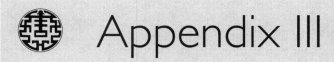

Appendix III

Vocabulary List

Guide to abbreviations in Lesson column

Sample abbreviation	Vocabulary location
2	Lesson 2 in *Listening & Speaking* book
2-SUPP	Lesson 2 in *Listening & Speaking* book, in "Supplementary Words" section
2-RW	Lesson 2 in *Reading & Writing* book

Characters & Pinyin	Part of Speech	English	Lesson
八 bā	Num	eight	2, 2-RW
吧 bā	N	bar, cafe	9, 13-RW
吧 ba	Part	(to make a mild imperative, to imply agreement or a degree of certainty, to express unwillingness or hesitation)	8, 9, 13-RW
白 bái	Adj	white; plain	9-RW
百 bǎi	Num	hundred	2, 2-RW
班 bān	N/Adj	class; shift; regularly-run	15-RW
半 bàn	Adj	half, partly	9, 15-RW

拌 bàn	V	to stir and mix (with sauce)	6-RW
办 bàn	V	to manage, to handle, to set up	13-RW
镑 bàng	Meas/N	pound	4-RW
办公室 bàngōngshì	N	office	8-SUPP
爆 bào	V	to quick-fry; to explode	5, 6-RW
八月 bāyuè	N	August	10
杯 bēi	Meas/N	cup, glass	5
北 běi	N	north	14-RW
北京 Běijīng	N	Beijing	8-SUPP
杯子 bēizi	N	cup	5-SUPP
币 bì	N	currency, money, coin	3, 3-RW
边 biān	N	side, edge	5, 12-RW
表 biǎo	N	form, chart	16-RW
别 bié	V/Adv	difference; don't	18-RW
宾 bīn	N	guest	11-RW
宾馆 bīnguǎn	N	hotel, guesthouse	6

冰 bīng	N/V	ice, to freeze		9-RW
饼 bǐng	N	fried bread		4, 5-RW
拨 bō	V	to dial		6
不 bù	Adv	no, not		2, 8-RW
步 bù	N/V	a step; to go on foot, to walk		15-RW
不对 búduì	Exp	incorrect, wrong		10
不客气 búkèqi	Exp	You're welcome.		6
不是 búshì	Exp	No, it is not.		2
不谢 búxie	Exp	Not at all. / You're welcome.		3
菜 cài	N	dish; vegetable		4, 5-RW
菜单 càidān	N	menu		5
餐 cān	N/V	meal; to eat		8-RW
操 cāo	V/N	to operate; exercise		16-RW
厕 cè	N	toilet		11-RW
厕所 cèsuǒ	N	bathroom, toilet		7
茶 chá	N	tea		5, 8-RW

差 chà	Adj/V	short of, wanting; to differ from	9
常常 chángcháng	Adv	often	9
炒 chǎo	V	to stir-fry	5, 6-RW
炒鸡蛋 chǎojīdàn	N	scrambled eggs	5
炒鸡丁 chǎojīdīng	N	stir-fried diced chicken with diced vegetables	5
叉子 chāzi	N	fork	5-SUPP
吃 chī	V	to eat	4, 9-RW
吃饭 chīfàn	VO	to eat a meal	4
吃素 chīsù	VO	to eat only vegetables (vegetarian)	5
出 chū	V	to go out, exit; to appear	14-RW
初 chū	N/Adj	beginning, elementary	17-RW
出生 chūshēng	V	to be born	10
床 chuáng	N	bed	7
床单 chuángdān	N	bed sheets	7
春 chūn	N	spring	17-RW
此 cǐ	Pron	here, this	14-RW

葱 cōng	N	green onion	5, 7-RW
葱爆 cōngbào	N	quick-fry with green onions	5
醋 cù	N	vinegar	5, 6-RW
打 dǎ	V	to make (a phone call); to hit, to beat; to play (ball)	6
打电话 dǎdiànhuà	VO	to make a phone call	6
打扫 dǎsǎo	V	to clean, to sweep	7
大 dà	Adj	big, large, major; age	8, 10, 12-RW
大门 dàmén	N	main entrance	8
大学 dàxué	N	university, college	8-SUPP
单 dān	Adj/N	single, bill	11-RW
蛋 dàn	N	egg	5-RW
道 dào	N	road, channel	14-RW
的 de	Part	(function word)	6
灯 dēng	N	light, lamp	7
等 děng	V	to wait	7
地 dì	N	earth, locality, field	13-RW

第 dì	Aux	(indicates an ordinal number)	16-RW
地区 dìqū	N	area, region	6
点 diǎn	N/V	o'clock; (decimal) point; to choose, to mark	9, 15-RW
店 diàn	N	shop, store	6, 9-RW
电 diàn	N/Adj	electricity; electric	10-RW
电话 diànhuà	N	telephone	6
电话卡 diànhuàkǎ	N	telephone card	6
电视 diànshì	N	television	10
电影 diànyǐng	N	movie	10
丁 dīng	N	cube, diced piece	5, 7-RW
东 dōng	N	east	14-RW
都 dōu	Adv	all, both	4
豆 dòu	N	beans, peas	7-RW
对 duì	Adj	right, correct; opposite	10, 12-RW
兑 duì	V	to exchange, to convert	4-RW
兑换单 duìhuàndān	N	exchange form	3-SUPP

对面 duìmiàn	Prep	on the opposite side, across the street	8
多大 duōda	Int	how old?	10
多少 duōshao	Int	how many? how much?	3
二 èr	Num	two	2, 2-RW
法学院 fǎxuéyuàn	N	law school	8-SUPP
翻译 fānyì	N	translator, interpreter; to translate, to interpret	10
饭 fàn	N	meal; cooked rice	4, 5-RW
饭馆(儿) fànguǎnr	N	restaurant	5
房 fáng	N	room, house	11-RW
房间 fángjiān	N	room	6
肥皂 féizào	N	soap	7
分 fēn	N	¥0.01, cent; minute	3, 6, 3-RW
分钟 fēnzhōng	N	minute	6
腐 fǔ	N/V	bean curd; to decay	7-RW
附近 fùjìn	Adj/Adv	nearby; in the vicinity of, closely	8
港 gǎng	N	port; Hong Kong (short form of 香港 Xiānggǎng)	4-RW

港币 Gǎngbì	N	Hong Kong dollar (HK$)		3-SUPP
告诉 gàosu	V	to tell, to inform, to let know		6
个 ge/gè	Meas	(measure word for people or things, and can be used to replace some other measure words)		3
给 gěi	Prep/V	to, for (when transferring something to someone); to give		6
跟 gēn	Prep	with		9
工 gōng	N	work; worker; skill		18-RW
公 gōng	N/Adj	public, state-owned		10-RW
宫保 gōngbǎo	N	a spicy, diced meat dish		5-SUPP
公司 gōngsī	N	company, corporation, firm		10
工作 gōngzuò	V/N	to work; work, job		10
瓜 guā	N	melon, gourd		7-RW
馆 guǎn	N	shop, hall		8-RW
贵 guì	Adj	expensive, valuable, honored		6
贵姓 guì xìng	Int	your surname, please?		6
国 guó	N	country		4-RW
过 guò	V	to pass, to cross; to celebrate, to spend (time), to go through		8, 10, 12-RW

过生日 guò shēngri	V	to celebrate a birthday	10
还 hái	Adv	in addition, still, yet	4
寒 hán	Adj	cold	17-RW
汉 hàn	N	Chinese	16-RW
汉语 Hànyǔ	N	Chinese language	9
好 hǎo	Adj	good, well, OK	3
好吧 hǎo ba	Exp	OK, all right	9
好吗 hǎo ma	Exp	Is it OK? Shall we?	9
号 hào	N	number, size; date	6, 10, 11-RW
行 háng/xíng	N/V/Adj	line, profession; to walk; OK	4-RW
喝 hē	V	to drink	5
和 hé	Conj	and	4
很 hěn	Adv	very, very much	4
红 hóng	Adj	red; symbol of luck	9-RW
后 hòu	Adj/Prep/ Adv	rear, back, the latter; behind, after	8, 12-RW
后边 hòubian	N	back, rear	8

后天 hòutiān	N	the day after tomorrow	10-SUPP
护 hù	V	to guard, to protect	18-RW
护照 hùzhào	N	passport	6-SUPP
花 huā	N/V	flower; to spend	9-RW
话 huà	N/V	word; to talk	10-RW
坏 huài	Adj/V	bad, broken, to become spoiled	7
坏了 huài le	Exp	to be out of order, to become spoiled	7
换 huàn	V	to exchange, to trade, to change	3, 4-RW
黄 huáng	Adj	yellow	10-RW
回 huí	V	to return, to go back	6
婚 hūn	N/V	marriage; to wed	18-RW
机 jī	N	machine, engine; opportunity	10-RW
鸡 jī	N	chicken	4, 5-RW
几 jǐ	Int/Adj	how many?; a few, several	9
加 jiā	V	to add; plus	2
家 jiā	N	home, family	10

假 jiǎ/jià	Adj/N	false; holiday, vacation	17-RW
间 jiān	N/Prep	room; between	11-RW
见 jiàn	V	to meet, to see, to call on	9
酱 jiàng	N/Adj	soy bean sauce, sauce, jam; cooked in soy sauce	6-RW
教 jiāo/jiào	V	to teach	8, 13-RW
椒 jiāo	N	hot pepper plant	7-RW
角 jiǎo	N	¥0.10; corner, horn	3, 3-RW
饺 jiǎo	N	dumpling with vegetable & meat stuffing	7-RW
叫 jiào	V	to be called, to call out	6
教学楼 jiàoxuélóu	N	classroom building	8
鸡蛋 jīdàn	N	egg	4
鸡蛋汤 jīdàntāng	N	egg-drop soup	4
鸡丁 jīdīng	N	diced chicken	5
几点 jǐdiǎn	Int	what time?	9
几号 jǐhào	Int	what date (of the month)? what number?	10
街 jiē	N	street	14-RW

节 jié	Meas/N	section, segment, period (of a class); festival, holiday	10, 16-RW
今 jīn	N	the present, today	17-RW
今年 jīnnián	N	this year	10
今天 jīntiān	N	today	10
进 jìn	V	to enter, to come in	5, 14-RW
禁 jìn	V/N	to forbid; prohibition	15-RW
京 jīng	N	capital; [Beijing]	14-RW
经过 jīngguò	V	to pass by, to pass through	8
境 jìng	N	border, territory, condition	18-RW
九 jiǔ	Num	nine	2, 2-RW
酒 jiǔ	N	liquor, wine	8-RW
桔 jú	N	orange, tangerine	8-RW
局 jú	N	bureau; gathering	10-RW
咖啡 kāfēi	N	coffee	5
卡 kǎ	N	card	6, 10-RW
开 kāi	V	to open; to set out; to turn on, to operate	15-RW

看 kàn/kān	V	to watch, to see; to look after	10
可 kě	N/Adv/V	co(la) (first character of 可乐 kělè); but; can, may	8-RW
可乐 kělè	N	cola (short for 可口可乐 Kěkǒu Kělè)	5, 8-RW
可能 kěnéng	V/Adj	may, might; possible	10
可以 kěyǐ	Aux/V	may, can; may be permitted to	7
课 kè	N	class, course	9, 16-RW
刻 kè	N	quarter of an hour, 15 minutes; a quarter	9, 15-RW
块 kuài	N/Meas	¥1.00 (colloquial form of 元 yuán), dollar; (measure word for things in chunks or solid pieces); chunk	2, 7, 3-RW
筷子 kuàizi	N	chopsticks	5-SUPP
辣 là	Adj	spicy, hot	4, 6-RW
来 lái	V	to bring; to come; to arrive	5
了 le	Part	(indicates a change of situation or completed action)	4
乐 lè	N/Adj	(co)la (second character of 可乐 kělè); happy	8-RW
冷 lěng	Adj/V	cold, frosty	9-RW
冷饮 lěngyǐn	N	cold drink(s)	5

里 lǐ	N/Meas	inside, inner; a Chinese unit of length	12-RW
凉 liáng	Adj/N	cool; cold	9-RW
两 liǎng	Num	two; a few	3, 3-RW
料 liào	N	material, ingredient	8-RW
零 (0) líng	Num	zero	2
龄 líng	N	age, duration	18-RW
留学生 liúxuéshēng	N	student studying abroad, foreign student	8-SUPP
六 liù	Num	six	2, 2-RW
楼 lóu	N	multi-story building; story, floor	11-RW
路 lù	N	road; route, journey	12-RW
绿 lǜ	Adj	green	9-RW
吗 ma	Part	(forms a question)	4
马 mǎ	N	horse	12-RW
买 mǎi	V	to buy	6, 10-RW
卖 mài	V	to sell	6, 10-RW
买单 mǎidān	N	bill/check (in a restaurant or bar)	5

马路 mǎlù	N	road, street	8
馒头 mántou	N	steamed bread, steamed bun	4
毛 máo	N	¥0.10 (colloquial of 角 jiǎo); a surname	3, 3-RW
毛巾 máojīn	N	towel	7
没 méi	Adv/V	not; to not have (short form of 没有 méiyǒu)	5, 16-RW
没有 méiyǒu	V	to not have	5
每 měi	Adj/Pron	every, each	10, 17-RW
每个 měige	Adj/Pron	every, each	10-SUPP
每个星期 měi ge xīngqī	Adv/Adj	every week, weekly	10-SUPP
每天 měi tiān	Adv/Adj	every day	10
美 měi	Adj/N	beautiful; America (short form of 美国 Měiguó)	4-RW
美国 Měiguó	N	United States	6
美国人 Měiguórén	N	American (person)	3-SUPP, 5
美元 Měiyuán	N	U.S. currency, dollar	3
门 mén	N	entrance, door, gate	8, 13-RW
米 mǐ	N	uncooked rice; meter	5-RW

面 miàn	N	noodle, flour		5-RW
面条 miàntiáo	N	noodles		4
米饭 mǐfàn	N	cooked rice		4
民 mín	N	people, citizen		4-RW
明 míng	N/Adj	tomorrow, next; bright		17-RW
名 míng	N	name; fame		18-RW
明年 míngnián	N	next year		10
明天 míngtiān	N	tomorrow		10
末 mò	N/Adj	end; powder; last		17-RW
哪 nǎ	Int	which? what?		3
哪个 nǎge	Int	which? which one?		7
哪年 nǎnián	Int	which year?		10
哪儿 nǎr	Int	where?		3
那 nà/nèi	Pron	that		3
那个 nà ge/nèi ge	Pron	that one		3
那儿 nàr	Adv	there	3-SUPP	

奶 nǎi	N	milk, breast	8-RW
男 nán	N	man, male	11-RW
南 nán	N	south	14-RW
呢 ne	Part	how about (you, this, that)?	3
内 nèi	Adj/Prep	inside, inner	15-RW
能 néng	Aux/V	can; to be able to	7
你 nǐ	Pron	you	2
你的 nǐ de	Pron	yours	7
你好 nǐ hǎo	Exp	Hello! How do you do!	3
你们 nǐmen	Pron	you (plural)	4
年 nián	N	year	10, 17-RW
您 nín	Pron	you (polite form)	4
您的 nínde	Pron	yours (polite form)	6
牛 niú	N	cow	4, 7-RW
牛肉 niúròu	N	beef	4
女 nǚ	N	woman, female	11-RW

欧 ōu	N	Europe (short form of 欧洲 Ōuzhōu)	4-RW
盘子 pánzi	N	plate	5-SUPP
旁 páng	N/Adj	side; nearby; other	12-RW
旁边 pángbian	N/Adv	side; beside, nearby	8
朋友 péngyou	N	friend	9
啤 pí	N	beer	9-RW
啤酒 píjiǔ	N	beer	5
片 piàn	Meas	slice, thin piece	5, 7-RW
瓶 píng	Meas	bottle	5
七 qī	Num	seven	2, 2-RW
期 qī	N/V	period; to expect	16-RW
起床 qǐchuáng	VO	to get up	9
汽车站 qìchēzhàn	N	bus stop	8-SUPP
千 qiān	Num	thousand	2-SUPP, 2-RW
签 qiān	V/N	to sign; label	18-RW
签字 qiānzì	VO	to sign, to affix a signature	3-SUPP

钱 qián	N	money, cash	3, 3-RW
前 qián	N/Adv/ Prep/Adj	front; forward; in front of; preceding	8, 12-RW
前边 qiánbian	Adv	in front, ahead	8
前天 qiántiān	N	the day before yesterday	10-SUPP
青 qīng	Adj	blue/green/black	9-RW
请 qǐng	V	please; to invite	3, 14-RW
请问 qǐngwèn	Exp	may I ask…	3
去 qù	V	to go; away (after a verb, indicating action directed away from the speaker); past, previous	7, 16-RW
去年 qùnián	N	last year	10-SUPP
人 rén	N	person, human	3-RW
人民 rénmín	N	people	3
人民币 Rénmínbì	N	"People's currency," Chinese currency (RMB, ¥)	3
肉 ròu	N	meat	4, 5-RW
入 rù	V	to enter, to join	14-RW
三 sān	Num	three	2, 2-RW
三刻 sānkè	N	three-quarters of an hour, 45 minutes	9

商 shāng	N	business; a surname	6, 10-RW
商店 shāngdiàn	N	a shop, store	6
上 shàng	Adj/V	first, upper; to go up, to get on	9, 11-RW
上班 shàngbān	V	to go to work, to go to the office	9
上个 shàng ge	Adj	previous, first part of	10-SUPP
上个星期 shàng ge xīngqī	N	last week	10-SUPP
上个月 shàng ge yuè	N	last month	10-SUPP
上课 shàngkè	V	to go to class, to teach a class	9
上午 shàngwǔ	N	morning	9
商学院 shāngxuéyuàn	N	business school	8-SUPP
烧 shāo	V	to stew, to cook, to roast	6-RW
勺子 sháozi	N	spoon	5-SUPP
谁 shéi/shuí	Int	who?	6
生 shēng	V/N/Adj	to give birth to, to be born, to grow; life; raw	10, 18-RW
生日 shēngrì	N	birthday	10
什么 shénme	Int	what?	4

十 shí	Num	ten	2, 2-RW
时 shí	N	time, the present time, hour	15-RW
是 shì	V/Adj	to be (am, is, are, was, were); yes, correct, right	2, 9-RW
室 shì	N	room; office	13-RW
市 shì	N	market; city	14-RW
是不是 shì búshì	Int	Is it? Are they?	2
收 shōu	V	to accept, to receive	3
手 shǒu	N	hand	10-RW
书 shū	N/V	book, document; to write	13-RW
数 shǔ	V	to count	2
暑 shǔ	N	heat, hot weather	17-RW
数 shù	N	number	2
双 shuāng	Adj/Meas	double, twin, pair	11-RW
书店 shūdiàn	N	bookstore	8
谁 shuí/shéi	Int	who?	6
水 shuǐ	N	water	5, 8-RW

睡觉 shuìjiào	V/VO	to go to bed, to sleep	9
睡午觉 shuì wǔjiào	VO	to take a noon-time nap	9-SUPP
丝 sī	N	threadlike, silk	7-RW
四 sì	Num	four	2, 2-RW
四月 sìyuè	N	April	10
送 sòng	V	to send, to deliver	7
素 sù	Adj/N	plain; vegetable	5, 7-RW
酸 suān	Adj	sour	4, 6-RW
酸辣汤 suānlàtāng	N	hot-and-sour soup	4
素菜 sùcài	N	vegetable dish	5
岁 suì	N	year of age, year old	10
所 suǒ	N/Meas	place; (measure word for buildings)	11-RW
宿舍 sùshè	N	dorm	8-SUPP
她 tā	Pron	she, her	6
台 tái	N	stand; (short form of 台湾 Taiwan)	4-RW
太 tài	Adv	too, excessively, extremely	6

汤 tāng	N	soup	4, 5-RW
糖 táng	N	sugar, sweets, candy	5, 6-RW
糖醋 tángcù	N	sweet-and-sour (things)	5
天 tiān	N	day	10, 17-RW
条 tiáo	Meas	strip; measure word for long, narrow things	7, 7-RW
通 tōng	V/Adj	to lead to, to go through; open	14-RW
头 tóu	N	head, chief, end	5-RW
图 tú	N	picture, map	13-RW
图书馆 túshūguǎn	N	library	8
外 wài	N/Adj	foreign country, the outside; external	3-RW
外币 wàibì	N	foreign currency	3
外国 wàiguó	N	foreign country	10
外国人 wàiguórén	N	foreigner	3-SUPP
外教 wàijiào	N	foreign teacher (short form of 外国教师 wàiguó jiàoshī)	8
外事处 wàishìchù	N	foreign affairs office	8-SUPP
丸 wán	N	ball, pill, pellet	9-RW

碗 wǎn	N	bowl	5-SUPP
晚 wǎn	N/Adj	evening; late	15-RW
晚饭 wǎnfàn		dinner	9-SUPP
万 wàn	Num	ten thousand	2-SUPP
网 wǎng	N	net, Internet	13-RW
网吧 wǎngbā	N	Internet cafe	8
往 wǎng/wàng	V/Prep	to go; toward, in the direction of	8, 12-RW
晚上 wǎnshang	N	evening, night	9
喂 wèi	Intj	Hello	6
位 wèi	N	place; position	18-RW
卫生纸 wèishēngzhǐ	N	toilet paper	7
文 wén	N	literature; writing	13-RW
问 wèn	V	to ask	3
我 wǒ	Pron	I, me	2
我的 wǒde	Pron	my, mine	6
我们 wǒmen	Pron	we, us	5

五 wǔ	Num	five	2, 2-RW
午 wǔ	N	noon	9, 15-RW
勿 wù	Adv	don't	14-RW
午饭 wǔfàn	N	lunch	9
西 xī	N	west	14-RW
息 xī	V	to rest	15-RW
习 xí	V/N	to practice, to be used to; habit	16-RW
洗 xǐ	V	to wash	10, 11-RW
系 xì	N	department (in a college)	8, 13-RW
虾 xiā	N	shrimp	7-RW
下 xià	V/Adv/ Prep/Adj	to go down, to get off; down, under, below; next	11-RW
下班 xiàbān	V	to get out of work, to go off duty	9
下个 xià ge	Adj	next, second, latter	10-SUPP
下个星期 xià ge xīngqī	N	next week	10-SUPP
下个月 xià ge yuè	N	next month	10-SUPP
下课 xiàkè	V	class is over, to dismiss class	9

先 xiān	Adv	first, before	5
现 xiàn	N	now, present	15-RW
现在 xiànzài	N	now, present	7
香 xiāng	Adj	fragrant, appetizing	9-RW
想 xiǎng	V	to want, to think	10
小 xiǎo	Adj	little, small, young	3
校 xiào	N	school	18-RW
小姐 xiǎojie	N	Miss, Ms., young lady	3
下午 xiàwǔ	N	afternoon	9
些 xiē	Adj/Adv	some, a few; a little	5
谢谢 xièxie	V	thank you	3
新 xīn	Adj	new	6, 17-RW
星 xīng	N	star; a bit	17-RW
行 xíng/háng	N/V/Adj	line, profession; to walk; OK	4-RW
姓 xìng	V/N	to be surnamed; surname, family name	6, 18-RW
性 xìng	N	sex; nature; gender	18-RW

星期 xīngqī	N	week	10
星期二 xīngqī'èr	N	Tuesday	10
星期几 xīngqījǐ	Int	what day of the week?	10
星期六 xīngqīliù	N	Saturday	10
星期日 xīngqīrì	N	Sunday	10
星期三 xīngqīsān	N	Wednesday	10
星期四 xīngqīsì	N	Thursday	10
星期天 xīngqītiān	N	Sunday	10-SUPP
星期五 xīngqīwǔ	N	Friday	10
星期一 xīngqīyī	N	Monday	10
修 xiū	V	to repair, to fix	7
休 xiū	V	to rest, to cease	15-RW
休息 xiūxi	V	to rest	9-SUPP, 10
洗衣服 xǐ yīfu	VO	to do laundry, to wash clothes	10
洗澡 xǐzǎo	VO	to take a shower, to take a bath	9
需要 xūyào	V	to need	7

学 xué	V	to study, to learn; school, knowledge	8, 13-RW
鸭 yā	N	duck	7-RW
要 yào	V	to want, would like, need	3
也 yě	Adv	also	2
业 yè	N	profession; estate	16-RW
一 yī	Num	one	2
以 yǐ	Prep/V	at, on, of, with, by; to use	16-RW
亿 yì	Num	billion (hundred million)	2-SUPP
一百 yìbǎi	Num	one hundred	2
(一)点儿 (yì)diǎnr	Adv	a little; some	5
衣服 yīfu	N	clothes, clothing	10
一共 yígòng	Adv	altogether, in total	5
以后 yǐhòu	Prep/Adv/ Conj	after; later on, afterwards; after	9
一会儿 yí huìr	Adv	in a moment, shortly, for a little while	7
衣架 yījià	N	hanger	7
一刻 yí kè	N	one quarter-hour, 15 minutes	9

姻 yīn	N	marriage; in-law	18-RW
银 yín	N//Adj	silver, relating to money	4-RW
饮 yǐn	N/V	a drink; to drink	8-RW
英 yīng	N	Britain (short form of 英国 Yīngguó)	4-RW
营 yíng	V	to operate, to run; to seek	16-RW
英国人 Yīngguórén	N	British person	5
英文 Yīngwén	N	English language	8
英文系 yīngwénxì	N	English Department	8
英语 Yīngyǔ	N	English language	8
银行 yínháng	N	bank	3
饮料 yǐnliào	N	drinks, beverages	5
一起 yìqǐ	Adv	together	9
以前 yǐqián	Prep/Adv/ Conj	prior to; ago; before	9-SUPP
医院 yīyuàn	N	hospital	8-SUPP
一直 yìzhí	Adv	straight, straight on, continuously	8
用 yòng	V	to use	6, 10-RW

由 yóu	N/Prep	reason; through	14-RW
油 yóu	N	oil, grease	6-RW
邮 yóu	N/V	post; to mail	10-RW
有 yǒu	V	to have	4, 10-RW
右 yòu	N/Adj	right; right-hand	8, 12-RW
右边 yòubian	N	right side	8
邮局 yóujú	N	post office	6
有时候 yǒushíhòu	Adv	sometimes, at times	9
鱼 yú	N	fish	4, 5-RW
语 yǔ	N	language, words	16-RW
元 yuán	N	¥1.00 (the basic unit of money), dollar	3, 3-RW
圆 yuán	N	¥1.00 (formal written form of 元 yuán), dollar	3, 3-RW
园 yuán	N	garden	6
远 yuǎn	Adj	far away, distant	8
月 yuè	N	month	10
在 zài	Prep/V	in, at; to be in, to be at, to exist	3, 10-RW

再 zài	Adv	again, still	6
再来 zài lái	Exp	come again, come back	7
早 zǎo	N/Adj	morning; early	15-RW
早饭 zǎofàn	N	breakfast	9
早上 zǎoshang	N	morning	9
怎么 zěnme	Adv/Int	how? in what way?	6
炸 zhá	V	to fry in oil, to deep fry	6-RW
找 zhǎo	V	to look for, to seek; to give change	6
照 zhào	V/N	to photograph; license	18-RW
这 zhè/zhèi	Pron	this	3
这边 zhèbian	Adv	this side, over here	5
这个 zhè ge/zhèi ge	Pron	this one; this	3
这个星期 zhè ge xīngqī	N	this week	10-SUPP
这个月 zhè ge yuè	N	this month	10-SUPP
蒸 zhēng	V	to steam	6-RW
正 zhēng/zhèng	N/Adj	first (in lunar calendar); upright; main	18-RW

证 zhèng	N/V	certification, proof; to prove	18-RW
这儿 zhèr	Adv	here	3-SUPP
这些 zhèxiē	Pron	these	5
汁 zhī	N	juice	8-RW
直 zhí	Adj	straight; vertical; frank	13-RW
职 zhí	N	job, position	18-RW
止 zhǐ	V	to prohibit, to stop	15-RW
址 zhǐ	N	location, site	18-RW
只有 zhǐyǒu	Adv/Conj	only; only if	10
中 zhōng	N	middle; China (short form of 中国 Zhōngguó)	4-RW
钟 zhōng	N	clock, o'clock	6
中国 Zhōngguó	N	China	3
中国银行 Zhōngguó Yínháng	N	Bank of China	3
中间 zhōngjiān	N/Prep	middle, center; in between	8
钟头 zhōngtóu	N	hour	10

中文 Zhōngwén	N	Chinese language	8
中文系 zhōngwénxì	N	Chinese Department	8
中午 zhōngwǔ	N	noon	9
周 zhōu	N	week; cycle	17-RW
周末 zhōumò	N	weekend	10
猪 zhū	N	pig	4
住 zhù	V	to live, to stay	7
转 zhuǎn/zhuàn	V	to turn; to change; to rotate	8, 12-RW
猪肉 zhūròu	N	pork	4
子 zǐ	N/Adj	son; small; seed	6-RW
自 zì	Pron/Prep	self; from	16-RW
走 zǒu	V	to walk, to go, to leave	8, 13-RW
昨 zuó	N	yesterday, past	17-RW
昨天 zuótiān	N	yesterday	10-SUPP
左 zuǒ	N/Adj	the left; left-hand	8, 12-RW
左边 zuǒbian	N	left side	8

坐 zuò	V	to sit	5
做 zuò	V	to do; to be, to act as	9
作 zuò	V	to do, make; to act as; to write	16-RW